THE WRITINGS & LIFE OF
GEORGE MEREDITH

A CENTENARY STUDY

By MARY STURGE GRETTON

J.P., B.Litt.

Author of ' A Corner of the Cotswolds'
' Burford Past and Present'
' Some English Rural
Problems '

HASKELL HOUSE PUBLISHERS Ltd.

Publishers of Scarce Scholarly Books

NEW YORK. N. Y. 10012

1970

First Published 1926

HASKELL HOUSE PUBLISHERS Lᴛᴅ.
Publishers of Scarce Scholarly Books
280 LAFAYETTE STREET
NEW YORK. N. Y. 10012

Library of Congress Catalog Card Number: 70-117580

Standard Book Number 8383-1013-3

Printed in the United States of America

PREFATORY NOTE

To Professor H. H. Joachim and Professor George Gordon of the University of Oxford, and to Professor S. E. Morison now of Harvard University, I owe the encouragements that have led to the publication of this book. I am much indebted to Mr. W. M. Meredith as an individual, and, as a publisher, he most generously offered me use of all the quotations I might wish to make from his father's writings.[1] The photograph reproduced as the frontispiece is the one given to me by George Meredith himself for similar use in 1907. Of knowledge gained from the chapters on Meredith's poems which Mr. Basil de Sélincourt wrote for my earlier book (long out of print) it is impossible to divest myself now, even if I wished to ; on the contrary I have used here some passages from one of those

[1] *By permission of Constable & Co. Ltd. and Charles Scribner's Sons, New York.*

Prefatory Note

chapters. Also I have employed again certain lights thrown for me upon *One of Our Conquerors* twenty years ago by Mrs. Basil de Sélincourt—' Anne Douglas Sedgwick '.

To Mr. Humphrey Milford and to Mr. Harold Murdock I owe the deep satisfaction of being able to produce this centenary study of the works of George Meredith under the auspices of two great Universities—Oxford and Harvard.

MARY STURGE GRETTON.

OXFORD,
    May 1926.

CONTENTS

                                                              PAGE

   I. Introduction to George Meredith's Writings   1

  II. Meredith's Early Life and First Writings ;
        1828–1859   15

 III. *The Ordeal of Richard Feverel* ; 1859–1860   29

  IV. *Evan Harrington* ; Events of 1860–1862 ;   44
        Modern Love, 1862   .   .   .   .

   V. *Poems of the English Roadside* ; *Sandra
        Belloni* ; 1862–1864   68

  VI. Marriage ; *Rhoda Fleming* ; 1864–1865   .   81

 VII. *Vittoria* ; International Affairs ; *Harry
        Richmond* ; 1865–1871   .   .   .   89

VIII. Events of the Early Seventies ; *Beauchamp's
        Career* ; 1870–1874   107

  IX. *The Idea of Comedy* ; *The Egoist* ; Short
        Stories ; 1877–1879   127

Contents

PAGE

X. *The Tragic Comedians*; Some Events
1881–1885; *Diana of the Crossways* . 148

XI. Poems of the Eighties 174

XII. *One of Our Conquerors; The Sage Enamoured and the Honest Lady*; 1889–1892 192

XIII. *Lord Ormont and His Aminta; The Amazing
Marriage*; 1892–1895 . . . 207

XIV. Some Thoughts in Conclusion; Last Years;
1895–1909 233

CHAPTER I

INTRODUCTION

THE ravine between 1913 and to-day, made by the war years, dwarfs into apparent similarity widely dissimilar men and events upon the far side of it. When I wrote my earlier book about George Meredith in 1907 it was not easy to picture the England of 1859 that had been scandalized by *Richard Feverel*; but to make the circumstances of the mid-nineteenth century evident now is immensely more difficult. The present generation—the generation of Michael of *The White Monkey*, with mind wholly formed in, and since, the world war—assumes so wide a divergence from conventions of the opening of the twentieth century even, that, to it, parental ideas appear not far removed from ideas of grandparents and great-grandparents. Viewed through a telescope, 1909 and 1859 look not very unlike. Changes that had brought to the eighteen-nineties a heaven and an earth undreamed of thirty years earlier are lost sight of to-day. Yet, in some degree at least, the steps, the gradations, of the just-past century have to be recovered, if only to equip literary and historic appreciation. And there are, surely, few better maps of the ground the English mind moved over between 1828 and 1909 than the writings of George Meredith.

A dozen years ago any emphasized personal note in such a book as this would have seemed to me out of place. But to-day reminiscences, with every other means at my call, must be summoned to strengthen the outline of George Meredith's figure to eyes the other side from him, and from myself, of the war gulf.

On the 22nd of May 1909 I was present at the Memorial Service held for him that morning in Westminster Abbey; the same afternoon I was with the mourners who laid his ashes in the cemetery at Dorking. My 1907 book about his work George Meredith had read through in manuscript. The photograph reproduced as frontispiece for that volume, and used in this volume also, was a gift from him to me. On the day of his eightieth birthday, 12 February 1908, I expressed so far as I was able, in the *Westminster Gazette*, what, at that moment, Mr. Meredith stood for, to me and my kind. It is what I felt and said then that I am setting myself to recapture and repeat for this Introduction. In its after chapters, the book is woven, I hope indissolubly, with details of the circumstances of Meredith's life not available at that time.

Fifty-two years before 1908 Meredith had admonished the hero of his first romance :

>Thou that dreamest an Event,
>While circumstance is but a waste of sand,
>Arise, take up thy fortunes in thy hand,
>And daily forward pitch thy tent.

Between the penning of those lines and 1908 he had published thirteen novels and nine volumes of verse, besides short stories and essays. He had been writing while Dickens and Thackeray were still writing; his first volume of verse had been published the year after *The Prelude* had appeared ; his first

volume of prose had preceded all George Eliot's
novels. Those facts were, I noted, remarkable enough.
But what was still more remarkable was that Meredith had worked on through the time of Henry James,
Maupassant, and Gorky, under the conditions these
represented, and had preserved his original impulse.
For, though he had proved in such works as *The
Ballad of Past Meridian* that he could, if he would,
sound the minor cadences to perfection, he had determinedly not represented episodes, however poignant,
as episodes merely, but set his characters and his
events against long-running horizons. His eyes on
mankind's future, he had correlated and compared;
and, at eighty years, to his mind, the sum of it all
was Hope. His beliefs had been born of his brain, not
of young blood; ' Our faith is ours, and comes not on
a tide ' he had written to John Morley. He was more
of a Radical at eighty years of age than he had been
in youth; and of his social and political ideas coming
generations, I hoped, might be at more pains than
his own had been to inquire; for when the political
development of the early twentieth century should
come to be estimated it well might be that he would
be seen as having predicted and inaugurated it. The
history of his Radicalism was written for us in *Beauchamp's Career.* ' Beauty ', he says there of his hero,
' plucked the heart from his breast. But he had
drunk of the *questioning* cup, that which denieth peace
to us, and projects us on the missionary search of
the How, the Wherefore, and the Why Not, ever
afterward. He questioned his justification, and
yours, for gratifying tastes in an ill-regulated world

of wrong-doing, suffering, sin, and bounties un-
righteously dispersed. He said " by and by " to pleasure ; battle to-day.' And the object of battle was the
bringing of beauty to the many instead of the few.
The course of that involved, and Meredith explicitly
recognized that it involved, an epoch of ugliness and
apparent loss—temporary supremacy of those ' that
fear not for the State when full the trough '. But
this—the travail of a new birth—he had seen as
inevitable ; for what was past recall, what we could
not, if we would, fall back upon, was the Old Order,
' the grand old Egoism that aforetime built the
House.' The day of progress in single file had gone.
The undiscovered lands were used up ; the system
of individuals pegging out claims must be discon-
tinued ; for the nineteenth-century possessor of
a diamond-mine dragged nations and nations' armies
in his train. At the end of the eighteen-nineties the
struggle of competitive interests had appeared to
be at its height ; but, to Meredith's vision, under-
neath all the foam and the ferment the current was
altering its course. A new tide was setting. New
ideals were at work. Society had not yet control of
its limbs, but at least it was recognizing itself as an
organism and would never again feel that life's
possibilities had been realized within it

> until from warmth of many breasts, that beat
> A temperate common music, sunlike heat
> The happiness not predatory sheds.

Society's watchword henceforth would be Community;
and the future Meredith saw as in the hands of those
who voluntarily united with forces moving in that

direction. But, because it is not possible to unite yourself voluntarily to what you do not perceive, I came here to Meredith's Word for the Rich, and it was to the rich and not to the poor that he mainly addressed himself. A more intimate knowledge of Nature and close rough-and-tumble with one's fellow-men—these, he said, are the groundwork for human learning ; and from these inherited wealth walls a man off. In *The Empty Purse* and in many other of his writings he pleaded with the materially fortunate few, ardently and at length ; not, as is commonly done, on behalf of their less-endowed fellows, but on behalf of their own immediate interests. The tide of democracy, he said, cannot be stayed ; but if those possessing present social advantages would but take their new place in the new day, and not continue to cling to obsolete privileges, the good they would get in exchange for those worn-out privileges would more than outweigh the loss of them ; so much more than outweigh, Meredith said, that as soon as the wealthy and powerful could be induced to see facts as they were, no doubt would remain in their minds as to relative values.

' By my faith,' he declares, ' there is feasting to come, . . . Revelations, delights !   .   .   .   .   .
.   .   .   .   .   . I can hear a faint crow
Of the cock of fresh mornings, far, far, yet distinct.'

And this declaration of faith, this assurance of the sound heart of things, was offered to our *fin de siècle* consciousness of capacity for feeling by a man of incomparable sensitiveness, a man who had faced the thickets of thought and tracked impalpable horrors of nerve and sensation down to their lair. With Lucy and Emilia, Carlo and Nesta and Carinthia, he had agonized and prevailed ; with Richard and Alvan, Lord Ormont and Nataly and Fleetwood, he agonized and had not prevailed. And in the darkness and the light he had read the same lesson. If we will relinquish claims to exclusive Paradises, in earth or in heaven, we shall find the sum of our experience the loss not of our hopes but of our fears.

That human existence is set thickly with tangles Meredith would have been the last to deny. But the unconquerable terrors, he told my generation, had birth in man's nerves, and not in the facts of experience. Fear—not old-fashioned cowardice, but nervousness, modern, imaginative, half-aesthetic—was our chief demon. All that was necessary was courage to face facts, to throw away the pseudo-spiritual, pseudo-poetic ; more courage and more, till the facts we shrank from revealed themselves to us as spirit and poetry incarnate. I pictured him that day standing clear against the horizon beyond the undergrowths and the thickets ; his figure a beacon and his voice thrilling us with encouragement—the only enduring kind of encouragement—that which knows its conditions as part of its promise :

> Enter these enchanted woods,
>   You who dare.
> Nothing harms beneath the leaves
> More than waves a swimmer cleaves
> Toss your heart up with the lark,
> Foot at peace with mouse and worm,
>   Fair you fare.

> Only at a dread of dark
> Quaver, and they quit their form:
> Thousand eyeballs under hoods
> Have you by the hair.
> *Enter these enchanted woods,*
> *You who dare.*

From this matter of Meredith's gospel I turned to the manner. He had proved himself to be a first-rate critic. His *Essay on Comedy* had been recognized as a lasting contribution to literary criticism. His articles in the *Fortnightly Review*, alone, had established the fact of his delicate literary judgements. His reviewing of other writers' work had been singularly sympathetic and appreciative ; but it had been more than that. It had been related to the possibilities of his art and to the whole body of that art's achievement, and abounded in illustrations drawn from the masters of literature. It was obvious, therefore, that Meredith possessed a very fine power of literary discrimination, and any consideration of his own methods must be based on recognition of this in spite of the fact that he had laid himself open to the charge of being prolix and uneclectic in his own work. The truth was that his multiform activity obscured the single-mindedness of his impulse. He had thought about Man and Man's destiny till he had perceived whole regions of possibility waiting to be claimed, and he made it the object of his life to nerve his fellows to enter upon the fullness of their inheritance. It may seem paradoxical that certain pages which would not have been published by lesser writers should have been passed by an author head and shoulders

above any but the masters. But the explanation is
to be found in Meredith's conviction that he had
a message to deliver, and in his willingness, at need,
to sacrifice other considerations to its delivery. *The
Empty Purse,* he wrote in a letter to me, ' is not poetry.
But I had to convey certain ideas that could not find
place in the novels.' He was unwaveringly sincere.
His writing at times is ludicrous from overcrowding
of its content ; but it never comes within sight of
bombast or pretension because its author never
experienced the smallest desire to make much out
of little. His novels and poems are glossaries on his
reading of life, and for Meredith every aspect of life
was a spiritual manifestation. Life, and the inter-
play of art upon life was his business, the development
of the soul his theme,

> How from flesh unto spirit man grows,
> Even here on the sod under sun.

' It is ', he said, ' the conscience residing in thoughtful-
ness I would appeal to,' and again, ' narrative is
nothing. It is the mere vehicle of philosophy. The
interest is in the idea which action serves to illustrate.'
Meredith's time believed the spiritual and material
forces of the world to be at war with each other.
Sentimental romance and so-called realism had been
the fruits of this vision. Meredith saw spirit and
matter unified ; and, in consequence, it was his
avowed aim as a novelist to eschew the ' rose-pink '
of sentiment and the ' alternative dirty-drab ' of the
realist. These two tendencies, in his day running
off at right angles, would, he said, ' fortified by
philosophy ' unite in a novelist's art that was worthy

the name—' honourable fiction, a fount of life, an aid to life, quick with our blood '—representation of man's nature as it is, ' real flesh, a soul born active ; wind-beaten, but ascending.' This was his own declared ideal, and, this perceived, the peculiarities of his style would be seen as direct outcome of it.

The most distinctive of those peculiarities is his constant, everyday, employment of metaphor. Where his contemporaries nailed a train of thought or a series of statements in the mind with a single comparison, Meredith indicates a dozen images which, taken in flying succession, combine, not merely to express his conclusion, but to reproduce the passage of his thought. Occasionally image may be piled upon image fantastically, but that is only very occasionally. His imagination plays over every object it lights on ; but the point to be specially noted is that it is even more vivid in illuminating generalizations than examples, more scintillating in abstract regions than in concrete. The torches of his metaphor race along unmapped paths—a poet's mind is penetrating psychological recesses and caverns, and the pathway behind it is aflame. The fourth division of *Modern Love* turns abruptly from narration to disquisition :

> All other joys of life he strove to warm,
> And magnify, and catch them to his lip:
> But they had suffered shipwreck with the ship,
> And gazed upon him sallow from the storm.
> Or if Delusion came, 'twas but to show
> The coming minute mock the one that went.
> Cold as a mountain in its star-pitched tent,
> Stood high Philosophy, less friend than foe:

Whom self-caged Passion, from its prison-bars,
Is always watching with a wondering hate.
Not till the fire is dying in the grate
Look we for any kinship with the stars
Oh, wisdom never comes when it is gold,
And the great price we pay for it full worth:
We have it only when we are half earth.
Little avails that coinage to the old!

Imagery here is, if anything, more abundant than in the mere narrative of the three previous stanzas of the poem. Every line is metaphorical, every generalization is pictorialized. And the result, for the reader, is an amazing simplification of complicated ideas. Not only the experience of this husband in *Modern Love*, but the reader's experience, and that of all men while their theories are at war with their actions, appears clarified—converted from mere experience into thought. The philosopher's gold is put in circulation. Meredith has coined it, and presented it to his fellows; freed it from its technical embedding, and given it an aspect to be recognized in future. More than that cannot be done. This is not coin of the market-place. Only those readers will perceive its purchasing power whom intellect enables, or circumstances compel, to seek food for the mind. Of Dudley Sowerby, in *One of our Conquerors*, Meredith has written : ' The internal state of a gentleman who detested intangible metaphor as heartily as the vulgarest of our gobble-gobbets hate it, metaphor only can describe ; for the reason that he had in him just something more than is within the compass of the meat-markets. He had—and had it not the

less because he fain would not have had—sufficient
stuff to furnish forth a soul's epic encounter between
Nature and Circumstance : and metaphor, simile,
analysis, all the fraternity of old lamps for lighting
our abysmal darkness, have to be rubbed that we
may get a glimpse of the fray.'

But, beyond the merely unintelligent, two large
classes of George Meredith's critics remained. The
first class consisted of those who in no way under-
estimated the importance of the problems with which
Meredith set himself to deal, but demanded that their
philosophy and their fiction should be served to them
in separate dishes. The novel, said they, was quite
unsuited to be a channel of ethical teaching. To say
that was, in Meredith's view, to sign the death-
warrant of fiction—' to demand of us truth to nature,
excluding Philosophy, is really to bid a pumpkin
caper.' He contended that, to be in any way credible,
a transcript of later nineteenth-century life must
portray the inner as well as the outer ; men's minds
were probing, mining, testing themselves and all
they encountered ; groping, individually and collectively, in search of new ideals and inspirations
on nebulous borderlands of knowledge ; appre-
hending laws for human existence that had, as yet,
no formulae. Intuitive discoverers—the poets—
had transcribed now and again some phrase of pure
truth ; but these isolated fragments had been
regarded by the nineteenth century as *objets d'art*,
adorable specimens for museums, rather than as vital
revelations. Meanwhile the rank and file had been
infected with those blank misgivings, those obstinate

questionings, which at the beginning of the century
had been confined to the poets. Consequently the
problem novel was in vogue. How, George Meredith
asked, could the chasm between muddy trapesings
and ' the shining table-lands ' be bridged except in
a novelist who should unite the poet's vision with
sturdy sense of social and political progress—accept
humanity with ' the stem, the thorns, the roots, and
the fat bedding of roses ' that in so doing he might
envisage its flower ?   The second class of objectors,
while sympathizing both with Meredith's themes
and his attitude to them, were alienated by obscurities
of style that seemed to them unworthy and even
perverse.   Why, they asked, should the man who
could write *Modern Love* and the *Hymn to Colour*
miss out connectives and relative pronouns, invert
conditional clauses, use adjectives as substantives or
substantives as adjectives ?   The explanation required by these objectors consists, mainly, in the
fact that Meredith, failing in the younger years of
his life to win an adequate public for his works,
took to writing for himself—to addressing his own
intelligence—and, in doing so, greatly overestimated
the agility of other people's minds. Small opportunity
was afforded to him at the outset of his work for
learning what degree of swiftness average intelligence
could bear, and, his own mind being abnormally
impatient of the obvious, it was of that knowledge
he stood particularly in need. His compression of
phrases and his omissions are overdone ; and his
habit of seizing one streak of colour for his subject
from a metaphor and instantly dropping that meta-

phor to snatch a gleam from another, is apt to rank
the comparisons, rather than the object that is being
compared, in the forefront of his reader's mind. But,
in the main, these are defects of excellences. Some
effort may be needed for following the exactitude of
Meredith's thought ; that is seldom apparent at
first sight ; yet of almost all his writings it may be
said that their exaltation and vitality is with us from
the outset. Brilliance and versatility of intellect
have been, mistakenly, supposed to be Meredith's
chief endowment. His inspiration, really, lies in
his poet's grasp, the intensity of realization with
which he holds his main issue and keeps it living, in
defiance of the web of complexity he for ever was
weaving every side of it—a web which must have
strangled any but the strongest heart-beat within.
In spite of the pauses by the way, returns for analysis
and counter-analysis, the flow of passion in his
compositions asserts itself, and, if the reader will
trust himself to that, will bear him triumphantly
over all the eddies and twistings. Upon first acquaintance, George Meredith's novels should be read at
speed without worrying at obstacles or digressions.
' Mrs. Mountstuart,' he says, ' detested the analysis
of her sentence. It had an outline in vagueness and
was flung out to be apprehended, not dissected.'
Once the central characters are felt, the reader will
be willing enough to go back and gather up details.
For it is only in connexion with minor characters
and comparatively extraneous issues that Meredith's
tiresomenesses occur. His taste faltered only in
situations that did not put full tax upon it. Where

the ground is most delicate he is most secure. In much of his work there is no obscurity at all, and the key to the more difficult of his novels and poems was always to be found in the simpler ones. To readers without the preconceived antagonism to his themes which Meredith had to encounter in his early contemporaries, difficulties in his style proved unenduring.

Now, in 1926, I find small need to labour the point that the obscurity of his style was overestimated by his contemporaries. Young readers will not comprehend his works having been condemned as obscure. Those works are simple in comparison with so much that is current to-day. Broadly speaking, English fiction before George Meredith, Robert Browning, and Henry James concerned itself with the defined, if not with the obvious. A fault of fiction now, in this time of cubism in nurseries, is a tendency to offer the unaccustomed as the profound. But, at any rate, novel-readers to-day are familiar with adumbrations—with conceptions only half chiselled out of the marble because of their intricacy.

CHAPTER II

OUTLINE OF MEREDITH'S EARLY LIFE AND FIRST WRITINGS

IN his lifetime, George Meredith liked it merely to be known that he was of Irish and Welsh descent. His grandfather—Melchisedek Meredith—though a naval outfitter of Portsmouth town, was a yeomanry officer, hunted, and was a welcome guest in many country houses of south-east Hampshire. Both Mr. and Mrs. Melchisedek Meredith, in fact, were very unusual people. Pictures of them are given to us in The Great Mel and Mrs. Mel of *Evan Harrington.* They had four beautiful daughters, all of whom married, in their own neighbourhood, advantageously [1]; and one son. That son—Augustus Armstrong Meredith—was George Meredith's father. Augustus Meredith, born in 1797, married—about 1824—Jane McNamara of West Point, Portsmouth. Jane Meredith died when the only child of this marriage, George Meredith, was five years old. Augustus Meredith, who never after the death of his mother ' Mrs. Mel ' was any use to the business, then drifted to London, leaving his tiny son in Portsmouth. During these years George Meredith was sent for a short time to a boarding-school in Portsmouth.

[1] The eldest—Anne Eliza—married Thomas Burley, banker, and afterwards Mayor of Portsmouth. The second—Louisa —married John Read, consul-general for the Azores. The third—Harriet—married John Hellyer, brewer. The youngest —Catherine Matilda—married Sir Samuel Burdon Ellis.

He learned little there : but two incidents of that time came to fruit in after years. The first of these was that some person at this school read aloud to the boys *The Arabian Nights* : the second was his acute nervous suffering from the length of Sunday church services—suffering real enough to make an indelible impression on his mind as can be seen from his letters to the Jessopps, of the year 1864, in regard to Sunday observances at the Norwich Grammar School.[1]

In August 1842, when George Meredith was fourteen years old, he was sent to a Moravian school at Neuwied on the Rhine. Of the upright gentle influences of this school any reader who cares to know may learn from Professor Henry Morley who, a few years before George Meredith, had been sent to it. There Meredith remained for two years. He then, in January 1844, returned to England and in January 1846 was articled to a Richard Stephen Charnock who, besides being a lawyer, was an antiquary and a person of literary taste.

Meredith, a youth now of eighteen years, lived at this period in very real poverty. Recreations other than walking and conversation were beyond his purse. As a conversationalist, however, his mark was being made. By those who had heard his talk he was introduced to Lord John Manners and Charles Dickens, and through this connexion *Household Words* and *Chambers's Journal* accepted and published some of his poems. He made also the acquaintance of a son of Thomas Love Peacock. Meredith and Ned Peacock walked to Brighton together and, in

[1] *Letters of George Meredith*, vol. i, p. 139.

Ned Peacock's lodging near by the British Museum, Meredith saw a good deal of Ned's fascinating young widow sister, Mary Ellen Nicolls, with her small child, Edith Nicolls.

On the 9th August 1849 George Meredith and Mrs. Nicolls were married in St. George's, Hanover Square. By means of a small legacy, which had just come to George Meredith from a Portsmouth relation, the newly married pair travelled and lived abroad for twelve months. Then they came back to Weybridge, which was two miles from Thomas Love Peacock's home at Lower Halliford. The next year—1851— saw the publication of *Poems by George Meredith* dedicated ' To Thomas Love Peacock, Esq., with the profound admiration and affectionate respect of his son-in-law.'

This volume is now very rare, but the whole of its contents, except one poem, appears in the thirty-first volume of Constable's Library Edition of Meredith's works, under the title of *Poems written in Early Youth*. The verses are boyish and give hints only of the measure of achievement soon to follow. They were, however, praised in a review by W. M. Rossetti, and more highly still by Charles Kingsley who in a quite re- markable fashion predicted their author's future success. No money came from this venture, however, and the Merediths being at the end of their financial resources, George Meredith accepted his father-in- law's offer of a home with him. So to Thomas Love Peacock's house Meredith and his wife moved in 1853; and there, on the 11th June of that year, Arthur Meredith was born. Shortly after, Peacock installed the father, mother, and child, in Vine Cottage, just across the Green from himself at Lower Halliford.

Temperamental differences had begun to divide George Meredith and his wife almost from the beginning ; and the chafing of these had of course been very much increased by poverty. Circumstances of this date give poignancy to a letter written by Meredith a few years after this to his close friend, Frederick Maxse, when Maxse was asking for sympathy in his own love-making ; ' Can you bear poverty for her ? Will she for you ? Can she, even if she would ? Think whether you are risking it, and remember that very few women bear it and retain their delicacy and charm. See whether you feel, not what we call love, but tenderness for her.' The degree of estrangement between George Meredith and his wife was considerable in the year 1853 ; but, probably largely for the host father-in-law's sake, then, a ' surface ' was being maintained just as in *Modern Love* it is maintained. The sound sagacity and mellowness of Peacock's character no doubt formed a stabilizing influence. In 1858, however, appearances were shattered. In that year Mrs. Meredith left her husband and went to Capri with Henry Wallis, the artist and picture-dealer. She came back later to live at Weybridge ; but she and George Meredith were never reunited. At his wife's flight, George Meredith claimed Arthur. He and the small boy moved off to London, and by some means or other they subsisted there till the end of 1859. Then they went to lodge in Esher where the father and child were discovered again by the Duff-Gordons, who induced Meredith to move to Copsham, to be close to them.

At the end of the year 1855 had appeared *The Shaving of Shagpat, Farina* following it in 1856. My limits of space forbid me to spend much on these two experiments. Yet for comprehending Meredith's work it is necessary to pay some attention to these his two first essays in styles of romance. George Eliot wrote of *The Shaving of Shagpat*, at its appearance, as ' a work of genius ', precious ' as an apple-tree among the trees of the wood '. Meredith himself, just before the end of his life, said of *The Shaving of Shagpat*, ' An Allegory is hateful to the English, I gave it clothing to conceal its frame ; but neither that nor the signification availed. Very few even of my friends have read the book, and of these I can count but two who have said a word in favour of it.' To look carefully for the reason that *The Shaving of Shagpat* was almost neglected from the time of George Eliot's two reviews in 1856 till the nineteen-hundreds might be instructive. English people, after all, have done a good deal of reading of *The Arabian Nights* ; England produced *The Pilgrim's Progress*. Perhaps the hour in the nineteenth century which *Shagpat* fell into was particularly unpropitious. None the less, there are surely few more engaging pictures in our later literary history than that of George Eliot ecstatically welcoming this extrava-ganza. May we not imagine her attempting to placate Mark Pattison with it, perhaps carrying it to him in the spirit in which one cross-word-puzzle enthusiast consults with another to-day ? For *The Shaving of Shagpat* attempted no less than a Reading of Life ; George Eliot found in it a man launching himself, even more freely than she was doing, on discussion of the universal. Christian, in *The Pilgrim's Progress*, is saving his own soul ; Shibli Bagarag, in *The Shaving of Shagpat*, sets out to save the world—is the Reformer.

The root idea of the allegory is plain enough. Shibli Bagarag stands for a reformer ; Shagpat is the abuse with which he is to contend. So much is plain to all. For detailed interpretation of the allegory readers should turn to *The Shaving of Shagpat ; Interpreted by James McKechnie*, published in 1900. Here I have not space to do more than set out three or four of the points, unstressed in Mr. McKechnie's book, which seem to me specially indicative of the line of Meredith's thought.

In the tale, the power of the genie Karaz is immense, and the heroine—Noorna—tells Shibli Bagarag of the genie's terrific schemes for the perversion of mankind, and his dire influence in her own life. Karaz seems to stand for perverted and misdirected forces which the man of wisdom must conquer to mould them to his purposes. When, in the tale, Noorna first summons Karaz she replies to her father's objections to her trying to make use of him :

> It is the sapiency of fools
> To shrink from handling evil tools,

and, through much danger and difficulty, Noorna subdues Karaz into the shape of an ass and dutifulness to her bidding. There is connexion between this idea and the fact that the waters of the Well of Paravid afford Shibli the kind of insight requisite for the management of men. On his return from this Well, Noorna welcomes her lover with the assertion that the first of his tasks is performed ; for he is able now to speak persuasively. She further replies to Shibli's question as to how he shall find his way alone to the City of Oolb, with the reminder that a drop of the water he carries will win from the herbs, stones, and sand replies to his questions. Yet two pages later we come on the injunction, ' Where men are, question not dumb things,' as the only response to his inquiries which Shibli can elicit from a city fountain. In the desert, that is, the bushes and stones would have answered ; but Shibli is now in a town. This, surely, is a characteristically Meredithian touch. No man ranked the magic of natural things higher than he ; but these were to be studied as a means to an end—that end, the comprehension of ourselves and our fellows. Meredith's seer is one who ' hither, thither, fares, close interthreading nature with our kind ', and in the last of his novels he condemned an out-of-doors enthusiast for ' studying abstract, and adoring surface Nature too exclusively to be aware of the manifestation of her spirit in the flesh '.[1]

Mr. McKechnie dwells of course upon the laugh of self-criticism that releases Shibli from the Hall of the Duping Brides. But the idea of the fruitfulness of laughter is everywhere in this allegory. The men who have been enslaved by the sorceress Goorelka,

[1] *The Amazing Marriage.*

and changed into birds at her pleasure, are freed into
men again as soon as Noorna has succeeded in keeping
them laughing uninterruptedly for the space of an
hour. The full virtue, too, of that cleansing laugh
in the Hall of the Duping Brides is only seen by us
as we analyse the nature of the experiences that
precede it. From the Realm of Rabesqurat, with
all its appeal to the senses, Shibli had made his escape.
Consequently, in Aklis, he has been safe from temptations offered by the fountains of jewels, the scented
halls, and marvellous feasts. It is only to the
blandishments of the damsels robed in colours of the
rising and setting sun, and waiting to crown and hail
him as their king, that he succumbs. And to them
he does not succumb till he has taken precautions
to test them and found no change in their beauty ;
as he wet their lips with his water from the Well they
had only each broken into luting and singing verses
descriptive of their various temperaments. One, light
as an antelope on the hills with timid graceful movements, sang

> Swiftness is mine, and I fly from the sordid ;

another, with arrows of fire in her eyes, and voice
like the passionate bulbul in the shadows of the moon,
sang, clasping her hands :

> Love is my life, and with love I live only,
> Give me life, lover, and leave me not lonely ;

whilst one came close up to Shibli, took him by the
hand and pierced him with her glance, singing :

> Were we not destined to meet by one planet ?
> Can a fate sever us ?   Can it, ah ! can it ?

Shibli is crowned and throned by the damsels in
a small inner chamber ; crowned, as he is presently to
discover, with asses' ears, and glued to his throne. His
charmers go out ; the door of his chamber is shut ;
and he is left to thick darkness, alone. He cannot
get free of his throne, but his struggles avail to move
it, with him sitting on it, out into the Hall of the
Brides. There the doors of ninety-eight recesses stand
open, and ninety-eight dupes like himself, solemn
and motionless on their thrones, are seen by him.
There appears small hope of freedom for Shibli ; many
of these monarchs are very old, and all appear to have
been long in their places. The sight of fellow dupes
might have given him cause for mirth. But Shibli
does not laugh, he does not even smile, till he suddenly
sees in a mirror himself with the crown on his forehead.
Then, not at the sight of the ludicrous appearance
of others, but at his own idiocy, he shakes the Hall
with his laughter. Here surely we have the first sight
of Meredith's Spirit of Comedy, and its fruitfulness.

Lastly there is the treatment of Rabesqurat—
Shibli's peering through the Veil of the Ferrying
Figure. Mr. McKechnie says of this Rabesqurat,
' In her nameless nature, it is forbidden to speak of
her. God seals the lips of those whom he lets peer
behind the veil.' This interpretation is at once too
definite and too vague. Shibli does indeed gasp the
name ' Rabesqurat ', but it is clear that what he sees
cannot be the Queen of Illusions as she was shown
earlier in the story. Sensuous enticements cannot
catch Shibli now ; it must therefore be impossible
to terrify him with revelation of the illusion of things

of the senses. The change in standpoint is subtle, but it is surely essential. At first the Queen of Illusions had pitted immediate satisfactions of sense against the life of the spirit, and for a while she had prevailed : ' The soul of Shibli Bagarag was blinded by Rabesqurat in the depths of the Enchanted Sea. She sang to him, luting deliriously ; and he was intoxicated with the blissfulness of his fortune, and took a lute and sang to her love-verses in praise of her, rhyming his rapture. Then they handed the goblet to each other and drank till they were on fire with the joy of things.' Temptation, then, took an elementary form ; illusions were presented as realities. The matter is vastly different now ; and the key to the difference is surely to be found in the title of the *Ferrying Figure*. The latest temptation is the very converse of the earlier wiles of Rabesqurat. The reformer, aflame with his mission, is suddenly confronted with the imminence of Death, and for the time being he is paralysed. He sees Life itself as Illusion. He ceases to be interested in his existence, and it is only by the friendship of Abarak and the affection of Noorna that the ashes of his spirit are rekindled. I dwell upon this point, because if there are readers who require to be convinced of Meredith's understanding of human life, they cannot do better than turn to three chapters, only eleven pages in all, of the allegory, ' The Veiled Figure ', ' The Bosom of Noorna ', and ' The Revival '. Shibli has been trained, tested, and fully equipped for his task ; his spells have been surrendered, his life truly dedicated, when this final disaster overtakes him. Connecting, as I believe we are intended to connect, the experience with Rabesqurat, it is shown to us as merely the swing of the pendulum, the old incapacity for separating illusion from reality, seen on its reverse side. So put, the truth seems evident enough ; but the discovery was Meredith's. For, in man's life as in *Shagpat*, the two forms of seduction lie far apart. The first is obvious and comes to all men ; the second is subtle and comes only to the spiritually-minded— those who have learned to sit lightly to the world, who have loosed the tenacity of their grasp on tangible things. It has been claimed that no genuine Contemplative forgets or neglects the details of his or her Order, and the extraordinary capacity for detail of such minds as St. Catherine of Siena's is instanced. But there is in existence, and there was far more in Meredith's day, a pseudo-mysticism which allows emphasis on transiency and mortality to paralyse the only means of expression of which man's spirit is assured. The familiar ' we will eat and drink, for to-morrow we die ' of the courtiers of Rabesqrat is complicated ; ' to-morrow we die ' is made the principal clause, and in the shadow of that all human effort is sunk to the level of eating and drinking.

When *Farina* was published, in 1857, the *Saturday Review* cavilled at the redundance of its language, attributing that fault to the influence of ' Mr. Ruskin, who has taught young writers to lay on their colours too bright and too thick.' The *Athenaeum* wrote more appreciatively of Meredith's powers in general, but, in regard to this particular book, the reviewer inclined to take with one hand what he had accorded

with the other. ' *Farina* ', he says, ' is a full-blooded
specimen of the nonsense of genius.' Actually the
story is a well-sustained rendering of romantic adventure in a medieval setting. We are told how Farina,
a youth of Cologne, who possesses all the courage of
his comrades, without their barbarous habits of
demonstrating it, wins the city's cynosure, daughter
of the wealthiest burgess, for his wife. This forms
the main motive. The purity of Farina's love and
the perfection of his courage are shown to be inter-
dependent, and the method by which his bride is
actually won introduces the ' second subject '.
Farina accompanies a monk, Gregory, who has an
appointment there with the Devil, to the summit of the
Drachenfels. With the youth as his witness, Gregory
encounters the Evil One. The Devil, feigning that
the monk is his conqueror, goes back to the nether
regions by way of Cologne. The smell of his exit
that he leaves there makes Cologne pestiferous ; and
the Kaiser, who is camping outside, cannot enter
the city. But Farina is a chemist, and he, escorting
the Kaiser, conquers the stench with the ' Eau de
Cologne ' which he has invented, and receives his
bride in reward. As to that bride's—Margarita's—
willingness there has for long been no question. For
she is of the order of women that Meredith loved ;
a girl with many boy-like characteristics, who uses
her eyes and her brain for the purpose of finding
realities and living in the light of them. The key
to her character is given in her reply to her Aunt
Lisbeth's warnings against natural depravity, ' where
I see no harm, Aunty, I shall think the good God is,

and where I see there's harm, I shall think Satan lurks.' Courage and tenderness are the qualities Margarita asked in her lover and as soon as she finds them in Farina, she loves him directly, openly, and with her whole heart. We see her first in the vineyards, dressed in a short blue gown with a scarlet bodice; her hair like ripe corn, and in it a saffron crocus stuck bell downwards. Her blue eyes smile frankly, but something as yet unstirred is in their depths—a sleeping dragon—which, because Margarita 'has not dallied with heroes in dreams', will spring up at need, will handle a sword in the den of the robbers, and face death unafraid. Wedded to her, Farina, when warehouses of false Farinas displaying imitations of his flasks rise round him, is able to laugh at 'the back-blows of Sathanas'. 'Fame and fortune', he mused, 'come from man and the world. Love is from heaven. We may be worthy and lose the first. We lose not love unless unworthy. Would ye know the true Farina? Look for him who walks under the seal of bliss; whose darling is forever his young sweet bride, leading him from snares, priming his soul with celestial freshness. There is no hypocrisy can ape that aspect.'

Though the tale of *Farina*—included now in the volume of *Chloe and other Stories*—is short, it has in it many of the essentials of Meredith's later works, and shows already his special faculty for combining pageant and problem. The tale's chief interest for us now must lie in the degree in which we find in it signs of Meredith's maturer mind. But to say this should not be to forget that it possesses a delicate quality of its own. The keynote of the story is the contrast between the monk, who by renouncing the joys of life falls a prey to the destructiveness of spiritual pride, and Farina, who, by his fearless welcome to all life offers, achieves the very conquest claimed by the ascetic. Neither *The Shaving of Shagpat* nor *Farina* may appeal to our tastes; we may dislike both of the styles Meredith was copying. Yet we cannot question his skill as an imitator, nor refuse to admit that the two tales possess a vitality unobscured by the mannerisms in which they are decked. They make it evident, too, that Meredith has views of his own to express—serious views—though not stated with obvious seriousness. Social reformation, for instance, is typified by a shave; thwacking epitomizes the spiritual discipline a reformer must undergo; and the natural fragrance of a life that overcomes the ascetic's slur on humanity is symbolized by the invention of eau-de-Cologne. Meredith, at twenty-eight years, has proved himself to have great agility in adopting foreign idioms. He is, we suspect, preparing himself to speak in his own. The wagging tongue, and the spell of vain longing which ties every faculty except the tongue, he has held up to our scorn. When he speaks for himself, he will, we imagine, speak of realities.

CHAPTER III

THE ORDEAL OF RICHARD FEVEREL

THOMAS HARDY has said since Meredith's death 'the man seems alive yet beside his green hill'. The scenery of Surrey colours all Meredith's writing; but it was in *The Ordeal of Richard Feverel* it was fixed on his canvas first and completely.

Actually the book was written in 1858 and 1859, the time when George Meredith with his tiny son was hiding from acquaintances in Chelsea lodgings. But that was the penning of its pages merely; the glowing heart of the story came from the summer Surrey of previous years. The relation of father and son in the tale was suggested to George Meredith's mind by Herbert Spencer's famous educational article in the *British Quarterly Review* for April 1858.

In this, the first of George Meredith's novels, there is no affectation of frivolity, no cloaking of earnestness. It does not contain the noblest of Meredith's creations, the emotional pitch is not so well sustained as in *Sandra Belloni*, but in its fusion of intellect and feeling it is perhaps the greatest of his works. The thought is brought into relation with the story, and in comparison with most of Meredith's novels, the book is free from side issues. The Feverels are brilliant, and in their mouths aphorisms are not out of place. Sir Austin Feverel, moreover, is just the kind of person who would commit his reflections to paper and publisher; and, in availing himself of this likeli-

hood, Meredith has obtained his background of commentary with unusual adroitness : ' Who rises from
prayer a better man, his prayer is answered ' ; ' When
we know ourselves fools, we are already something
better ' ; ' For this reason so many fall from God
who have attained to Him ; that they cling to Him
with their Weakness, not with their Strength ' ;
' Nature is not all dust, but a living portion of the
spheres ; in aspiration it is our error to despise her,
forgetting that through Nature only can we ascend.'
Those who are familiar with Meredith's thought
through his subsequent works recognize these sayings
as expressions of his most individual conviction,
but in *Richard Feverel* they appear woven into the
fabric of the plot and related to the character of
Sir Austin.

A good deal of interest and much light on George
Meredith's development can be obtained by comparing *Richard Feverel* as we have it now with its
earliest form.   Some persons profess to prefer the
story as it stood in the first edition.   I think it is
impossible to agree with them.   The alterations made
for the second edition [1] are indeed the best of wit-
nesses to Meredith's power of self-criticism.   Detailed
accounts of the many lady admirers of The Pilgrim's
Scrip, Sir Austin's forefathers, Sir Miles Papworth's
ideas and appearance, even Richard's earliest birth-
days, and Ripton Thompson's invitation to Raynham
and arrival there, were so much dead-weight on the
story.   The only value of these details is that they
familiarize us with the early stages of Meredith's

---

[1] Not called for till nineteen years later.

conception of some of his characters. Of Sir Austin we glean a good deal from the earlier, less vigorous, portrait. We hear more of his popularity before his wife's flight; we see him from that hour, when Richard is four years of age, fussy and over-anxious, even superstitious in his guardianship; and we realize a fact which, though really it is stated in the story as it now stands, may be missed by readers unfamiliar with the general line of Meredith's thought —that the baronet's calamity, instead of making a philosopher of him as he supposed, had led him to dwell on ' The Ordeal' of the Feverels, and to look on his experience as unique. Here, too, we find the explanation of what many of us must have found puzzling—how Sir Austin, with his instinct for nobleness, could have chosen Adrian rather than Austin as Richard's tutor—' Austin had offended against the Baronet's main crochet, that to ally oneself randomly was to be guilty of a crime before Heaven greater than the crime it sought to extinguish.' [1]   Later editions merely inform us that Austin Wentworth does not live with his wife; but in the earliest edition his uncle's attitude is presented with greater explicitness: ' Think, Madam,' the baronet says to Lady Blandish, ' think that he, a young man of excellent qualities, has madly disinherited his future. I do not forgive him. The nobler he, the worse his folly. I do not forgive him.' Again, Benson's curious and somewhat offensive position in the household is explained fully also and on similar grounds: the butler had represented

---

[1] 1859 edition, vol. i, p. 54.

himself as being unfortunate in marriage, and as
sharing Sir Austin's views of the nature of women.
In fact the degree of emphasis laid upon this particular subject in the first edition of the book was
tasteless ; and Meredith later in life evidently felt
it to be so. The value of the first edition to us is in
bringing out the truth that Sir Austin, while he
supposes himself detached and judicial, is really
twisted in mind by his suffering. His Pilgrim's
Scrip is a mine of much wisdom ; but pride and self-
pity prevent Sir Austin from applying his knowledge.
' The direct application of an aphorism,' we are told,
' was unpopular at Raynham.' Yet Sir Austin is by
no means a fool : Meredith describes him, at the
crucial moment of his relationship to Richard, as
' a fine mind, a fine heart, at the bounds of a nature
not great '. That he is aware of his own lack of
humour is stated explicitly ; and real intellect is
necessary for such awareness ; belief in their perception of the comic being deeply rooted in most un-
humorous persons. Admirable is it also to keep
a brave face to the world—when one is hurt to refuse
to whimper—and in this task Sir Austin is only too
successful. Above the common run of men in
character, he comes triumphantly out of all the
common testings of conduct : he is cruelly deceived,
but deception does not make him wrathful or vindictive. In the normal ways of life his bearing is
blameless ; but he aspires to something greater than
the normal, and, in thus aspiring, encounters his
Ordeal. He attempts to play Providence to Richard,
and to stand to Lady Blandish for Wisdom incarnate.

His sorrow has taught him something of mankind, but little or nothing of himself. When Richard breaks from his control, he questions not the nature of that control, but the soundness of humanity; when Lady Blandish pleads for Richard's forgiveness, he imagines himself great-minded in maintaining a frigid detachment. ' By the springs of Richard's future, his father sat: and the devil said to him, "Only be quiet: do nothing: resolutely do nothing: your object now is to keep a brave face to the world, so that all may know you superior to this human nature that has deceived you." Further the devil whispered, "And your System—if you would be brave to the world, have courage to cast the dream of it out of you: relinquish an impossible project; see it as it is— dead: too good for men!" "Aye!" muttered the baronet, " all who would save them perish on the Cross!" ' ' How ', here comments Sir Austin's creator, ' are we to distinguish the dark chief of the Manichaeans when he talks our own thoughts to us ? ' Chiefly, perhaps, by tendency to lay the blame for our personal misfortune on the shortcomings of humanity; above all, by any inclination to seek great parallels for our private experiences, and in debasing words of holy association to betray our ignorance of spiritual values.

' Expediency is man's wisdom, doing right is God's.' On this truth, apprehended intellectually by Sir Austin Feverel, his nephew Austin Wentworth intuitively acts. At our introduction to Austin he is ostracized, not for the error of his youth but for its atonement—' " married his mother's housemaid,"

whispered Mrs. Doria '—and for his championship of
the poor. We first see him in his interview, after the
rick-burning, with Tom Bakewell. Unlike the rest of
the Feverels, Austin is not brilliant : he avoids
preaching at Richard, but that avoidance is instinctive rather than reasoned ; for he falls into the error
of attempting to paint, to Richard, Tom Bakewell in
prison. Richard's sense of the ludicrous is much
keener than Austin's and pictures of Tom's loutish-
ness do not forward the argument. Nevertheless
Austin's purpose is fulfilled. Richard accompanies
him to make confession to the farmer. And this first
scene is characteristic of the way Austin Wentworth's
single-mindedness brushes brain-spun obstacles, like
cobwebs, from his path. Lucy's admirers, half-
hearted and whole-hearted alike, hesitate and man-
œuvre for months as to how she is to be brought into
her father-in-law's presence ; Austin returns from
five years' absence in the tropics to learn Lucy's
address and her predicament from Adrian in Picca-
dilly, and by nightfall Lucy and her child are at
Raynham. ' I have brought Richard's wife, sir,'
with a joking question as to his own exact relationship
to the baby, is Austin's introduction of the pair ;
and when the newcomers are accepted and borne off
to their sleeping apartments, ' a person you take to
at once ' is his only rejoinder to the baronet's surprise
at Lucy's attractiveness. It is Austin who brings
Bessie Berry's long-truant husband to her feet. It
is his presence Lady Blandish entreats when Lucy
lies dead in a French cabaret ; the tragedy had
darkened beyond human help, but she feels that

Austin's presence may rekindle faith in the onlookers. Where Austin is, we feel that all will go well, just as where Adrian is, all will go wrong. The fact that Austin's appearances in the tale are short and infrequent matters not much, because he survives as a permanent feature in Meredith's work. In Bessie Berry's reminder to Lucy on the night of their arrival at Raynham to pray blessings on the simple-speaking gentleman who does much because he says little, not Austin Wentworth alone but Meredith's favourite type of masculine character is indicated.

Misapprehension as to the value he set upon mere intellect, of which I spoke in my Introductory Chapter, led some of Meredith's contemporaries to suggest that the character of Adrian Harley portrayed Meredith's ideal, if it was not a picture of himself. It is indeed a cardinal point of Meredith's teaching that intellect is the lodestar of the spiritual man— that feeling, however sweet and pure it may be, is an inadequate director of conduct. But, surely, in all teaching it is needful to make certain assumptions; and that capacity for emotion is the very basis of human equipment is a fact on which Meredith supposed it was not necessary to insist. Adrian is the wittiest person in the book, and all the Feverels are witty : to Austin's plea of urgency when Richard is being implicated in the rick-burning, ' The boy's fate is being decided now,' Adrian yawns out ' So is everybody's, my dear Austin ' ; and to Richard's repeated assertions that Lucy had done all in her power to put off the marriage, he rejoins, ' Not all ! not all. She could have shaved her head, for instance.'

Meredith allows us, in spite of Adrian's cleverness,
no doubt as to his baseness of nature. 'Adrian
Harley,' he tells us, 'had mastered his philosophy
at the early age of one-and-twenty. Many of us
would be glad to say the same at that age twice-told,
but they carry in their breasts a burden with which
Adrian's was not loaded. Mrs. Doria was nearly
right about his heart. A singular mishap had un-
seated that organ and shaken it down to his stomach.'
Lucy, when his name is mentioned to her, asks
whether he is good. 'Good?' says Richard. 'He's
very fond of eating, that's all I know about Adrian.'
He was in the habit of making jokes 'delicately not
decent, though so delicately so that it was not decent
to perceive it'. He was a person to be reckoned
with on account of his wits; but he was detestable,
and it would hardly be possible for him to be more
heartily detested than he is by his author.

Richard's cousin Clare is the least satisfactory
feature in the tale. Her death, intended to heighten
the tragic atmosphere, is not convincing. We are
told, in connexion with Richard's home-coming after
his separation from his family, that his consciousness
of the duel to take place on the morrow made the
value of each human relationship piercingly clear
to him; 'the thought of the leaden bullet dispersed
all unrealities.' This, we feel, is as it should be, and
as it actually is, when any of us comes close to death.
But it surely cuts at the root of the story of Clare.
She has decided to die; she has even taken the
poison; yet she writes on in her diary of love and
longing for Richard, writes till bodily torment is

shown in the penmanship. Even allowing for a strong vein of morbidity, this seems unnatural. Clare had the inhibitions at least of a gentlewoman. Probably her unassuming nature would not have ·written the diary at all ; but, even if she had, in health, it is certain that, in the presence of death, she was more likely to have destroyed, than to have prolonged, her outpouring. The action which is described to us is the action, not of the person who commits suicide, but of the person who talks about committing it.

I have said that the first edition of *The Ordeal* contained a good deal that was tasteless ; but what is remarkable to note is that the portions, later so wisely discarded, concerned only subsidiary matters. The infantine Richard, Mrs. Doria, Sir Austin's admirers, Benson, Ripton Thompson, the old doctor and Mrs. Grandison, were the characters affected. The heart of the tale, its heights and depths, were all as we know them now. Nothing has been taken from the scene of Richard's meeting with Lucy, and nothing has been added to it. The river that opened out to the founts of the world was the same as it is now, magical with the genuine magic of dawn. Gleam of water and earth, glint of heron and king-fisher, song of skylark and blackbird, with scent of meadows—these things were caught, exquisite and unmarred, from the first. The idyll of young love with its background of midsummer flowers, came from the hand of the author perfect as now. ' Golden lie the meadows : golden run the streams : red gold is on the pine-stems. The sun is coming down to earth, and the fields and the waters shout to him golden shouts. He comes, and his heralds run before him and touch the leaves of oaks, and planes, and beeches, lucid green, and the pine-stems redder gold ; leaving brightest foot-prints upon thickly-weeded banks, where the foxglove's last upper bells incline, and bramble-shoots wander amid moist rich herbage. The plumes of the woodland are alight ; and beyond them over the open, 'tis a race with the long-thrown shadows ; a race across the heath and up the hills, till, at the farthest bourne of mounted eastern cloud, the heralds of the sun lay rosy fingers, and rest. Sweet are the shy recesses of the woodland. The ray treads softly there. A film athwart the pathway quivers, many-hued, against purple shade fragrant with warm pines, deep moss-beds, feathery ferns. The little brown squirrel drops tail and leaps ; the inmost bird is startled to a chance tuneless note. From silence unto silence things move.'

' With its background,' did I say ? The phrase is strangely superficial. Speech or action of the lovers occupies the least part of the pages in which the marvel of their love is revealed to us. The greater part is devoted to the pageant of earth, the glorious procession of the hours. It was for some time customary to believe that, whatever else Meredith might have done or left undone, he had accomplished in *The Egoist* what he came to do. But that book is hardly more than a sketch—an exercise—beside the full-blooded wealth of *Richard Feverel*. *Richard Feverel, Sandra Belloni, Harry Richmond, One of our Conquerors,* are not perfected artistically ; they

contain subsidiary characters and events that are
out of drawing. Classic they are not in their form—
compared with French and Italian models, and with
some novels even of our own race, their form is
uncouth—but by virtue of their poetic vision. We
feel in Lucy and Sandra and Roy that the dust of
humanity has been breathed on by a creatoı. Their
dramas include the unuttered part of our speech.
Meredith has given us later, and more intellectualized,
statements of kinship between Earth and her young ;
but in *The Ordeal of Richard Feverel* is its spontaneous,
earliest, expression, broad in appeal because grounded
on the commonest human experience—an expression,
moreover, of which prose in no previous hands had
proved itself capable ; ' The tide of colour had ebbed
from the upper sky. In the west the sea of sunken
fire draws back ; and the stars leap forth, and
tremble, and retire before the advancing moon, who
slips the silver train of cloud from her shoulders, and,
with her foot upon the pine-tops, surveys heaven.
" Lucy, did you never dream of meeting me ? " " O
Richard ! yes ; for I remembered you." " Lucy !
and did you pray that we might meet ? " " I did ! "
Young as when she looked upon the lovers in Paradise,
the fair Immortal journeys onward. Fronting her,
it is not night but veiled day. Full half the sky is
flushed. Not darkness ; not day : but the nuptials
of the two. " My own ! for ever ! you are pledged to
me ? Whisper ! " He hears the delicious music.
" And you are mine ? " A soft beam travels to the
fern-covert under the pine-woods where they sit ;
for answer he has her eyes : turned to him an instant,

timidly fluttering over the depths of his, and down-
cast ; but through her eyes her soul is naked to him.
" Lucy ! my bride ! my life ! " The night-jar spins
his dark monotony on the branch of the pine. A soft
beam travels round them and listens to their hearts.'

The maturity of workmanship is striking enough
here ; and it is no less manifest in the chapter called
' Nursing the Devil '—psychologically perhaps the
finest in the book. But it is on the tragic heights
of the story that the art is supreme ; above all in
the scene that Robert Louis Stevenson called the
strongest written since Shakespeare—Richard's last
meeting with, and parting from, Lucy—and in
Richard's wanderings in the forest when he has just
learned that he is a father. Richard is in Nassau with
Lady Judith Felle, his sentimentalist friend, when
Austin arrives and tells him of the birth of his
son. This news scatters Richard's vapours. He
starts off by himself into the forest when a great
storm is imminent. And mountain and woodland,
sultry silence, and rush and thunder of tempest
Meredith employs as orchestral accompaniment to a
man's wakening spirit. Despite Richard's anguished
repentance, alone there amid the grandeurs and
mysteries of storm in the mountains, he, the sole
representative of humanity, feels himself greater than
they ; ' A father . . . A child.' To render an idea of
this, the latter part of the forty-third chapter of *The
Ordeal of Richard Feverel*, musical images only may
serve. The whole is a Concerto. Up and up through
the forest, on to the mountain, Richard presses. From
the breathless heat to the moment the rain slashes

the leaves and his face, with the drumming of thunder
and the quivering darts of the lightning, on to the
vast deluge of water sating the gorging earth, is a
fortissimo passage, issuing, as Meredith's descriptions
of spiritual tempest so often afterwards were to issue,
in the piano movement of dawn and dawn's level
spaciousness—the baby leveret's tongue going over
the palm of the hand Richard had thrust with it
into his breast, the peasants' wayside Virgin and
Child, and the cornlands of the plain. And this
scene, moving though it be, is but an antechamber
to the scene where Richard at last has returned to his
wife, the scene where the light in Lucy's eyes is like
the light on a moving wave—changeful yet constantly
radiant—and Richard again and again asking if his
confession has been understood receives one answer
only, and that in its turn no answer but a question :
' " You love me ! Richard ?   My husband ! you
love me ? "   " Yes, I have never loved, I never shall
love, woman but you."   " Darling ! Kiss me ! "
" Have you understood what I have told you ? "
" Kiss me," she said. He did not join lips.   " I have
come to-night to ask your forgiveness." Her answer
was still " Kiss me."   " Can you forgive a man so
base ? "   " But you love me, Richard ? "   " Yes :
I can say that before God. I love you, and I have
betrayed you, and am unworthy of you—not worthy
to touch your hand, to kneel at your feet, to breathe
the same air with you." Her eyes shone brilliantly.
" You love me ! you love me ! darling ! "   And as
one who has sailed through dark fears into daylight,
she said, " My husband ! my husband ! my darling !

you will never leave me ?   We shall never be parted again ?"'   Of the immediate blighting of Lucy's hopes, of the terror of the parting, and the tragic outcome of it all, the book itself only may speak. The incidents belong to a level where there is no place for language that is not inspired.   We may question the artistic justifiability of events so heart-tearing ; but there can be no question as to the exaltation of style in which they are treated.   We are reminded of the comment of James Thomson's friend on another work of Meredith's, ' Here truly are words that if you prick them would bleed.'

The Ordeal of Richard Feverel is not a wholly satisfactory book.   The writer's sense of the tragedy of human existence is so keen that it borders on cruelty. Self-slain, his characters seem not the less almost hounded to ruin.   But to realize the greatness of the book, we need only to reflect how intolerable the story would become if shrunk to the canvas of an inferior writer.   We may not find the story like-able ; but we cannot, unless we are idiots, read and be blind to its power.   In view of this first of his novels we might question whether the author's outlook on life will grow broad-based enough to support his burden of sensitiveness ; but we know him already as a poet and not a transcriber—one who who is not boxed in with his characters but sees them against a great background of earth and of air.

Knowing, as we now know, the circumstances of George Meredith's life at this date, it is clear to us that he had lavished his own experience on this book. That he was chilled—badly chilled—by the critics' reception of it was inevitable. *The Times* alone among the leading reviews greeted it with genuine consideration. The *Athenaeum*, the *Saturday Review*, and the *Spectator* condemned it out of hand. The novel was preached against from certain pulpits, a fact that in our day would afford it the best of advertisements, but sixty-five years ago proved damning ; though Mudie's had purchased three hundred copies of it for their Library they withdrew the book from circulation. Meredith at this time was living at Copsham with Arthur, who was now between seven and eight years ; and was heavily troubled by illness from a chronic weakness of digestion which he strove to combat by indefatigable walking. At this time he accepted journalist work on an Ipswich newspaper, agreeing to send it a leading article and two columns of news-notes every week for a payment of about £200 a year. Nearly twenty years were to pass before a second edition of *Richard Feverel* was to be called for. In 1859 and 1860 it did less than nothing to add to the material wealth of its author. It did, however, bring enrichments of other kinds. From Thomas Carlyle it elicited first the ejaculation 'This man's no fule', and afterwards friendship ; and it brought Meredith into closer touch with Maxse, the Jessopps,[1] Monckton Milnes, Swinburne, and the Rossettis.

[1] Jessopp wrote that he and his fellow-undergraduates at Cambridge at this time were ranking Meredith second only to Tennyson.

CHAPTER IV

EVAN HARRINGTON
EVENTS OF 1860–1862
MODERN LOVE, 1862

WHEN George Meredith had gone to lodge at Esher, in 1859, in order to be near Frederick Maxse, he had already begun writing *Evan Harrington*; and by February of 1860 it was appearing as a serial in *Once a Week*. Those who have not read any of Meredith's books are often advised to begin with *Evan Harrington*. But such advice ought not to be given without the reminder that, though very diverting, this book is not to be ranked with most of Meredith's other novels in the riches it has to offer its reader. Being Meredith's, its playfulness is of course wise; but the situations of it depend upon circumstances that are accidental. The circumstances are, no doubt, in some measure, and to some extent, the circumstances of Meredith's father's house in Portsmouth.

The story is of a tailor's son, who, with the instincts and upbringing of a gentleman, finds himself, at his father's death, bound to the family business by debt. His mother—a remarkable woman—belonged to the professional classes, but Evan Harrington's distinction comes to him from his father. When the tale opens, his father, the Great Mel, is no longer living; but the whole story is saturated by his presence. Though neither his vice nor his virtue are on quite so heroic a scale as Roy Richmond's, Melchisedec Harrington and Roy meet in a common disdainfulness of money combined with requisition of the society and the circumstances that money affords ; ' Mr. Melchisedec was a tailor, and he kept horses ; he was a tailor, and he had gallant adventures ; he was a tailor, and he shook hands with his customers. Finally, he was a tradesman, and was never known to have sent in a bill.' Through his life he had managed to maintain a bearing of respect towards his wife, but the task had been difficult to him, owing to what he felt to be her sordid concern with details of business, her addiction to picking up the pence as he squandered the pounds. His four children—three daughters and one son—had been in their youth as far as was possible removed from the taint of the shop ; and, when the story begins, each of the daughters is assured of some social importance through marriage, while, under the eldest sister's tutelage, Evan, a lad of seventeen, waiting a commission in the army, spends the hours that are not devoted to gentlemanly lounging in his brother-in-law's brewery toying with the figures of big balances.

To the extravagance of the eldest sister who has obtained a Portuguese Count for her husband—the Countess de Saldar de Sancorvo, as by the end of the book she has come to style herself—we are first introduced when, in company with Evan and her husband, she has attached herself to a diplomatist's party fleeing from Lisbon to London. The Government sloop bringing this party is boarded in the Thames by Goren, a tailor, who brings Evan news of his father's death : ' I'm going down to-night,' Goren announces, ' to take care of the shop. He 's to be

buried in his old uniform. You had better come with
me by the night-coach, if you would see the last of
him, young man.' The Countess is sincerely affected,
but the word 'shop' may have been overheard and
must be retrieved! After a moment's strained
silence, the situation is saved by her outcry: 'In his
uniform'. Melchisedec had been in the Militia!
She is a master of intrigue; and on her own ground
it is not possible to outwit her, but she is, of course,
outwitted in the end by the one factor she has
no weapons to deal with—disinterested affection.
Failure, however, teaches Louisa de Saldar nothing
except to change her tactics. The book ends with
a letter Louisa writes to her sister, from Rome:
' *You* think that you have quite conquered the dread-
fulness of our origin. I smile at you! I know it to be
impossible for the Protestant heresy to offer a shade
of consolation. Earthly born, it rather *encourages*
earthly distinctions. It is the sweet Sovereign Pontiff
alone who gathers all in his arms, not excepting
tailors.' The Countess, Jack Raikes, the Great Mel,
and Tom Cogglesby make up a fantastic background
to throw into prominence the naturalness of Rose
Jocelyn—Rose being drawn from Meredith's young
friend of this period, Janet Duff-Gordon. And yet,
collectively, these eccentrics, and not Rose or her
lover, form the special feature of this tale. It is in
Tom with Andrew at the Aurora, interviewing Lady
Jocelyn, schooling the pretenders, that Meredith's
most individual thought finds expression. Here we
have the Comic Spirit lying in wait for impostors.
Cogglesby's mind teems with whimsical notions for

the correction of pretenders, ideas not vindictive, but salutary—born of a child heart and a full-grown intelligence. Perhaps nowhere else in Meredith's writings is his reading of life, his faith in earth's training of those who are teachable—those who are fools for a season only—better expressed than it is here, in its earliest form. The final form Meredith gave to the same teaching, in *The Empty Purse*, I have spoken of already.

Love-sick and engrossed in his own sorrows, Evan comes on a woman in extremity by the side of the road. ' A misery beyond our own,' comments Evan's author, ' is a wholesome picture for youth, and though we may not for the moment compare the deep with the lower deep, we, if we have a heart for outer sorrows, can forget ourselves in it. Evan had just been accusing the heavens of conspiracy to disgrace him. Those patient heavens had listened as is their wont. They had viewed, and had not been disordered by, his mental frenzies. It is certainly hard that they do not come down to us, and condescend to tell us what they mean, and be dumbfounded by the perspicuity of our arguments—the arguments, for instance, that they have not fashioned us for the science of the shears, and do yet impel us to wield them. Nevertheless, they to whom mortal life has ceased to be a long matter perceive that our appeals for conviction are answered—now and then very closely upon the call. When we have cast off the scales of hope and fancy, and surrender our claims on mad chance, it is given us to see that some plan is working out : that the heavens, icy as they are to the

pangs of our blood, have been throughout speaking
to our souls ; and, according to the strength there
existing, we learn to comprehend them.   But their
language is an element of Time, whom primarily we
have to know.'   Those two last sentences contain in
them   the   cardinal   points   of   Meredith's   creed.
Throughout his work he is pleading with his fellow-
men to learn to be what he calls Sons of Time—that is,
to cease clinging to the past in any respect.   Inex-
perienced youth, in Meredith's view, represents
nothing but energy—potentiality—either for good or
evil.   He says of Evan, at the opening of Evan's
career, ' Most youths are like Pope's women ; they
have no character at all.'   And, in respect to another
of his young heroes, Meredith is even more explicit.
In *Sandra Belloni* he says : ' Wilfrid was a gallant
fellow, with good stuff in him.   But he was young.
Ponder on that pregnant word, for you are about to
see him grow.   He was less a coxcomb than shame-
faced and sentimental ; and one may have these
qualities and be a coxcomb to boot, and yet be a
gallant fellow.   And harsh, exacting, double-dealing,
and I know not what besides, in youth.   The question
asked by Nature is " Has he the heart to take and
keep an impression ? "   For, if he has, circumstances
will force him on and carve the figure of a brave man
out of that mass of contradictions.'   But at what
cost ?   At the price commonly of many of the things
he began by holding dearest ; whereat he reproaches
Nature his creator, and Circumstance his sculptor,
forgetful that their sole object is to mould him into
a man.   At the close of *Evan Harrington* it is clear

that this task has been performed. Of Evan's honesty and manliness there can be no longer question. He has clearly ' struck earth ' ; that is, he will in future base his efforts and ambitions on the realities of his circumstance and his character. Necessity of this ' saving grasp in the stern-exact ' is the fundamental belief of the creator of General Ople and Clotilde von Rüdiger. A man or woman whose aspirations are not rooted in fact, the primary fact being the limitations of their own character, is, in Meredith's eyes, useless and worse. A man must learn to see himself as he is, divested of all false and adventitious aids ; recognize exactly the nature of the raw material he has to work with, before he can begin to weave the fabric of a life. In early days the shuttle may seem to cross and recross at a great pace ; but, until a pattern has been chosen and the threads selected and controlled to some determined end, there will be no issue upon the loom. For possibilities of self-deception, of unreality, of confusion between sentiment and emotion, are almost unlimited ; Evan, reclining in his chariot on the way to his father's funeral, believing himself to be meditating on Love and Death, sees a halo cast about tailordom and is able to despise the world that looks down on it. Yet immediately, when he finds he has not money enough for his postillion's tip, and sees himself consequently lowered in the postillion's estimation, his pride is up in arms ! Still the Fates that are at work moulding Evan find that he can ' take an impression '. He has been deceiving himself and attitudinizing before Rose Jocelyn, and this experience with the postillion gives

E

him a first glimpse of this : ' From the vague sense
of being an impostor he awoke to the fact that
he was likewise a fool.' None the less, a few hours
after, he informs his father's creditors, in the lordliest
fashion, that he will pay their accounts to the uttermost farthing, without pausing either to estimate the
number of the bills or the sacrifice of himself
involved in paying them. At this point, Chapter VI
of the book, Evan has shown himself capable of
' taking an impression '—self-criticism. The sterner
task of learning to maintain an impression—to
remodel habits—lay in front of him yet. But that
lesson he masters in the space of the story. And the
reason of Evan's learning it with swiftness Meredith
would have us inquire. In part that is due, of course,
to the soundness of Evan's temperament ; but, in the
main, it is the result of the weight of the sculptor's
hand on him—the fact that Evan's circumstances
are the very opposite of the circumstances of Lord
Fleetwood, Willoughby Patterne, or the gilded youth
of *The Empty Purse.*

In the spring of 1860 George Meredith was in the
hands of the Esher doctor, and writing with great
regret to Janet Duff-Gordon that he was too unwell
to be at her wedding. He was very depressed and
talking then about giving up Copsham and going back
to live in London lodgings. May of the next year,
however, 1861, finds him writing to Janet that he is
still at Copsham Cottage, and is remaining there for
Arthur's sake. And, alluding to *Evan Harrington*, the
same letter says, ' Talking of Rose, did you see *The
Saturday Review* ? It says you are a heroine who

deserves to be a heroine. Yet I think I missed you.'
There are many signs in Meredith's letters in this
spring, of 1861, that he was recovering his cheerful-
ness. He reports that he has three works in hand,
Sandra Belloni being the most advanced of the three.
He tells Janet Ross that Arthur is developing excellently, and is so ceaseless an interest that the idea
of the child's having to be sent to boarding-school
will not bear thinking about.

From July to mid-September 1861 George Meredith
took Arthur, who was now eight years old, abroad ;
travelling by way of Ostend and the Rhine to Zurich,
Innsbruck, and the Tyrol, on to Venice, and home
again through Paris. From Meran he was able to
write to friends in England that he was revelling in
thirty-mile walks beneath a hot sun ; and he greatly
enjoyed Venice where he and Arthur were bathing
constantly in the Adriatic. Altogether the change
and rest of these months proved most beneficial, and,
by the end of that September, again from Copsham
and again to Janet Ross, Meredith was able to report
much improved health. Moreover, one aspect of
a long strain was about to be relaxed. Ever since the
autumn of 1858, that is, for three years past, George
Meredith had devoted himself passionately to Arthur,
being nurse, governess, everything, to the child. But,
unfortunately for that child's later peace of mind, he
was adored by both—separated—parents ; and
Mrs. George Meredith had been for some time now
living, in great unhappiness of spirit, not far from
Copsham. In this September, of 1861, she was
mortally ill. And the same letter to Janet Ross, which

I have just been quoting from, reports, ' Arthur is
now at Weybridge seeing his mother daily.' To have
had to look at such a situation through the child's
mind must, of course, have doubled the intensity of
it to Meredith. In October 1861 Mrs. Meredith died.
At the date of her death George Meredith was in
Norfolk, and actually he did not hear of the decease
till some days later. Of the effect of the news, when
it came to him, we have fortunately been allowed to
learn from a letter then written to William Hardman.[1]
From accusation of complacency that letter entirely
releases George Meredith. The spirit of it is the spirit
of the closing stanza of *Modern Love*. Indeed allusion,
other than George Meredith's own, to this event of
1861 would be avoided here except for that event's
concern with years that were still to come. Inevitably, in regard to the child of this ill-starred marriage,
complication appeared to have been removed now
that there was no longer any necessity for his having
at times to pass from one parent's house to another ;
George Meredith thought and spoke of Arthur at this
time as having become entirely his own ; and,
especially in the next two or three years, he lavished
on the little boy thought and devotion such as very
few children can have experienced. Yet the ingrati-
tude and ungraciousness towards his father that was
soon after this to spring up in Arthur, and to grow
with his years, probably had here, in 1861, its root.
I do not for one moment mean to suggest that the
small boy ' sided with ' his mother. Nothing so
simple as to be comprised in a child's consciousness is

[1] *Letters of George Meredith*, 19 Oct. 1861.

in the least likely to have occurred. But children
who experience parental affections that are obviously
separated, therefore necessarily to the child eye con-
taining an element of rivalry, cannot develop as other
children develop. For they are always taking shelter
in a sanctuary where the discipline of childlike
experiences cannot get at them. Whatever the
general atmosphere surrounding them, from any
small particular adversity or discomfort in the home
of one parent they retreat imaginatively to the home
of the other. To be a child is, necessarily, to be at
moments displeased with experience. From such
momentary displeasures the child of parents living
under one roof normally entertains no idea of refuge—
of sanctuary—short of the blessedness of becoming
grown-up. Thus he comes, more or less quickly
according to his temperament, into tolerable relations
with his comrades and their way of life. In any case
Arthur Meredith's would not have been an easy-
going temperament. But can we not picture his
childish wilfulness, after this October 1861, as taking
shelter always, from any gainsayings, in memories of
that alluring, exciting, April-shower-like mother, who
had somehow been prostrated and brought to final
disappearance by the father who remained to talk
about working hard at Latin and washing one's
hands ? In the month following Mrs. Meredith's
death, November 1861, Augustus Jessopp, at that
time Head Master of King Edward VI Grammar
School, Norwich, visited George Meredith and his
small son at Copsham Cottage, and, while there,
Jessopp proposed that he should undertake to educate

Arthur entirely at his own expense and under his own eye. The offer as to payment Meredith felt himself unable to accept, but so impressed was he with Jessopp's ability and character, and Mrs. Jessopp's attraction and kindliness, that he there and then agreed—terrible as he foresaw the wrench to himself was to be—to send the child to school at Norwich in a year's time.

The close of this year—1861—saw *The Tragedy of Modern Love* in the printer's hands ; it was given to the public in the following May. The noble letter in which Swinburne replied to an attack on *Modern Love* in the *Spectator* is almost hackneyed to-day ; yet some words of it familiarity is without power to stale : ' A more perfect piece of writing no man alive has ever turned out than " We saw the swallows gathering in the sky " ' ; ' Work of such subtle strength, such depth of delicate power, such passionate and various beauty ; in some points, as it seems to me, a poem above the aim and beyond the reach of any but its author.' The sixty years since the letter was written have brought the literary critics, at any rate, to Swinburne's estimate of the poem. Unfortunately, however, these years have witnessed no sufficiently careful contradiction of a minor matter in regard to which Swinburne's lead led astray. It is, of course, permissible for a poet to speak to poets of the sections of *Modern Love* as ' sonnets ', just as a painter, speaking to fellow-painters, might call a red blue, relying on the dominant quality being as obvious to his hearers as to himself. But to the general public undoubtedly the word used by Swinburne has been misleading. For, in employing that word, we are obscuring an essential refinement of the poem. The fifty divisions of *Modern Love* contain sixteen lines each, and these lines are divided into quatrains ; the first and fourth, and the second and third, lines of each quatrain rhyming. All that these sections have in common with a sonnet is the length of their lines and the pithiness of their expression ; they have nothing of the sonnet's particularity and finality of structure. In many cases, notably in XVIII and XIX, XXI and XXII, XXIII and XXIV, the last four lines of one section might quite well be placed above the first four lines of the next. In part the poem is pure narrative, so the treatment of the theme necessarily is continuous. The divisions are roughly comparable to chapters, serviceable in allowing for alterations of scale or changes of aspect, but sometimes merely divisions. For the author's object in thus simplifying and modifying the sonnet-form has been to secure, with the variety afforded by division, a flowing— almost a processional—continuity of dramatic effect ; a continuity which would have been destroyed by greater completeness of structure in the divisions. This would have seemed too evident to require emphasis, were it not that as comparatively lately as 1890 a literary critic, after discussing the question at length, came to an opposite conclusion. But the value of the whole argument which led to Mr. Le Gallienne's conclusion appears to me to be vitiated by his underlying supposition that it was necessary for him to prove that Meredith could, if he would, have written *Modern Love* in sonnets. In face of the fact that Meredith has written elsewhere a number of most admirable sonnets that supposition is surely irrelevant.

Such obscurities as there are in *Modern Love* are almost entirely unavoidable. In phrasing, the poem is not obscure ; the wording is straight-forward, and direct. The difficulty lies in the matter. What, we should ask ourselves, exactly is the theme of the poem ? It is concerned certainly with the usual three—husband and wife and lover—and their acts are of a commonplace kind. But these acts and deeds are not the theme of the poem ; they form a ground-work, merely, that is more or less taken for granted. The subject is the knowledge and insight arising out of elements earthy enough in themselves. Difficulty of comprehension by the reader comes, if it comes, from the fact that the poems of *Modern Love* give, not a narrative, but a running commentary on a narrative which is told by implication mainly. More-over, many sections of the poem are, even in isolation, so beautiful that the reader is prone to be content with his vision of separate elevations without seeking for the ground-plan to relate the whole. Yet, because the writer of the poem definitely makes demand on the reader's mind to carry such a ground-plan, there is no escape from the necessity of its provision. But the task of supplying it in words is not alluring, because what such a plan has to do is to provide the elements that are not poetic. There is risk, too, in the attempt, for it was no part of George Meredith's intention to provide placards that whoso runs may read. He indeed prefaced the first edition of *Modern Love* with the words :

> This is not meat
> For little people or for fools.

It should be admitted at once, also, that the story
Meredith's genius has raised in this poem to tragic
heights is not of any great quality in itself.   In the
tale as it actually is, 'he'—the husband—is maddened
by discovering that his wife is spiritually unfaithful
to him, and in love with another man.   The story is
told throughout by the husband, who describes his II
reactions of feeling beneath the mask of a polite
demeanour—how at one moment he is enraged by his
wife's grace of manner and bearing into regarding her
as the vilest spot on a blackened earth, at another
strives in reactionary gentleness for magnanimity,
while, in remorse for the sterner feeling, he learns the
bitterness of his pain.   From thought of his wife he III
turns to 'the man', her would-be lover, first to call
him negligible—a worm to be trodden under foot—
then to writhe at perceiving him irradiated by her
gaze.   The power of that look to glorify what it falls
upon drives him half to curse the beauty that holds
him bound, and in the same breath to question why
he forgoes its sweetness—' It cannot be such harm
on her cool brow to put a kiss ? '   But no !   He has
been deceived.   The object of his love exists no longer
—' The hour has struck, though I heard not the bell ! '
He attempts to turn for relief to other interests, but IV
life has gone out of them all.   Illusion or diversion
lasts for a moment only, and his agony revives the
fiercer for its lull.   But he is not a sensational being
merely ;   half the poignancy of his suffering lies in the
fact that he is at war with himself, that his intellect
has a standard to which his senses prevent his actions
from conforming.   Into his wife's interest in household

v affairs he reads hypocrisy and scheming. He sees her
using her beauty as a net to ensnare him, and the
acute temptation of allurements by which he is
almost beguiled increases his bitterness. But she is
befooled too. Her eyes have been trained for shining,
not for use ; and they have not enough penetration
to discover the existence of a force that avails to
restrain the impulse she is appealing to. A chance
vi endearment of his is met, not with womanly shame,
but in a way only suggesting that her love has cooled.
With sounds of midnight sobbing in his ears, knowing
her feeling to be intensely alive and only the object
of it changed, he stings himself with thoughts of her
wantonness and the title her conduct might warrant
him in using. But all the while this agony is beneath
the surface, an under-current at the fireside where
they sit—' she laughing at a quiet joke ' ; for the
decencies and appearances of their outward life are
being strenuously upheld. Her radiant beauty pur-
sues him continually, driving him to believe that her
vii faithlessness is the more criminal for having avoided
the most obvious expression, and taunting him from
viii one extreme of feeling to the other. At times he is
passionately pitiful, caring more for her lost loyalty
ix than his own pain, at others marvelling that the wild
beast within him does not seek its brute revenge.
x Where, and what, he asks, is the nature of the crime
that has brought this wretchedness upon him ?
Merely that he has slept and wakened ; and, waking,
xi refused to act upon the impulse of a dream. The
beauty of earth and returning spring serve only to
intensify his consciousness of loss. In imagination,

he points his wife to the golden west, where ' in an
amber cradle near the sun's decline ' is lying the
infant love that she has slain. But the greatest of xii
her crimes is not that she has stripped him of the
future. She has robbed him of the past. For it is
a reality no longer, though the shadow of its mockery
goes with him for ever. And here again the contrast xiii
of man's life with nature's makes itself felt. Why, he
asks, can we not learn of her whose care is for seasons,
not eternities, and who bestows no regret upon her
fading flowers ? Life lived only in the present, without memory or desire—that surely must be the way of
escape ? And yet the analogy is not complete ; for
the human rose—love rooted and renewed in sense—
is a flower of surpassing loveliness.

A fourth actor in the drama is now introduced.
The husband turns for solace to a friend, known xiv
throughout the rest of the poem as ' My Lady ', in
distinction from ' Madam ', his wife. The immediate
result is that contempt for ' Madam ' is aroused by
signs in her of a veering fit and jealous renewal of
affection. The new element of scorn is perhaps
intended to serve as an excuse for the next poem, xv
surely one of the most unpleasant in the series, in
which he awakes his wife from sleep, or from pretence
of sleep, to show two letters both in her own hand-
writing, one written long ago to himself, the other
lately : ' The words are very like : the name is new.'
Meanwhile, they still appear to the world as the
happiest of couples. His wife shines as a hostess and xvii
his guests are excellently entertained—' they see no
ghost '. This game of hiding the skeleton has a

certain zest, and the players begin to admire one
another's acting. The husband at times is tempted to
xviii envy the uncomplicated lives of the country bumpkins
dancing on the green, till he reflects upon the sources
xix of their enjoyment. Torn by conflicting impulses
towards gentleness and cruelty—reflecting that to
escape from inconstancy to one person by forging
vows to another is the road by which love drifts into
the market-place—he concludes that the only really
enviable condition must be that of the village idiot.
His attempt to view the situation impartially is
xx further complicated by the discovery of ' a wanton-
scented tress ' in a long-unused desk of his own, which
serves as reminder of deeds for which he, on his side,
stands in need of forgiveness. One evening a friend,
xxi who has scoffed at lovers hitherto, stands with them
on the lawn and begins the tale of his ' most wondrous
she ' and, ' convinced that words of wedded lovers
must bring good,' entreats their blessing. Forgetful
for an instant of his presence, their eyes meet in
horror. Then, recovering themselves quickly, they
give what he requires. But a moment later the wife
falls fainting to the ground, and the irony of the
bystander's probable reading of the event flashes
through her husband's mind. Soon it becomes evident
to him that she is hovering on the brink of some con-
xxii fession ; her movements are irresolute and tentative,
and once she stands before him in tears. But words
do not come. Her husband will not question, and
a gulf that seems impassable yawns between them.
xxiii Christmas arrives, and they are together at a country-
house overflowing with guests ; they share an attic

bedroom, and from the accident that brings them thus
together, learn how wide the estrangement, how deep
the mortification, that divides them. The husband
sets himself to freeze with the freezing cold outside :
it is more than his wife can bear. But he steels his xxiv
heart against tokens of her suffering. Her offence
he knows is only against love ; but he persuades
himself that a grosser sin would have been easier to
forgive. He will not be propitiated by signs of her
unhappiness, though he has to call loudly on his sense
of dignity in order to dismiss his longing. He
questions her ironically as to her distaste for a French
novel she is reading. Why does she pronounce it xxv
unnatural ? because the heroine is compelled to
choose between her husband and her lover, and
chooses as a woman should ?—unromantic possibly,
but true to life ! Musing on the serpent which has
taken love's place in his heart, any consciousness of xxvi
his own shortcoming forsakes him, and he thinks only
of the wrong which has been done to him. It is, he
believes, still possible to pardon the doer of it, if she
will fling her cowardice to the winds and make frank
and free confession ; but he has no help to lend her :
' You that made love bleed, you must bear all the
venom of his tooth.'

Nervous and unstrung, he determines to fall in with
his doctor's prescription, and seek distraction where- xxvii
ever it may offer. He is inclined to be on good terms
with the devil, who proves friendly when no other
helper is at hand, and he begins a period of dalliance
with ' My Lady ' in a spirit of pure devilry and xxviii
cynicism. But because in the past he has had true

feeling for this friend, his flirtation develops into something more vital, and the reality of his outcry xxix on what the relation is not, bears witness to his having discovered exactly what it is. In the light of this knowledge he begins to generalize on the xxx growth and nature of love. But though his words are brilliant, his estimate is cynical, and amounts to little that he has not formulated earlier in the poem. Love is a dream—an illusion—and, when it crumbles, man does best to recognize himself as an animal with animal desires, and employ his intelligence in satisfying them scientifically. He will act on this theory, and, instead of sentimental romancing, a relentless statement of fact shall form his sonnet to his lady's xxxi eyes. But she is intelligent and capable of facing realities ; she has ' that rare gift to beauty, Common Sense ', and in their intercourse his spirit begins to revive. Relationship with her has unique qualities. He insists repeatedly on this, trying hard to persuade himself that it embraces and supersedes the old. He xxxii dwells on the charms that his Lady adds to her intelligence ; and yet the truth will out. The episode is unreal ; he knows that his wife's place has not been taken ; he is inwardly torn and fretted by living memories, ' a dying something never dead.' He begins to suspect that the cure for the wound his wife has dealt does not lie with any other member of her sex. But his nerves are all on edge, and he extracts a certain cynical pleasure from the thought of her xxxiii bewilderment should she chance to spy upon his letters to his friend ; he writes in one of these of the inevitable soiling to a man's soul incurred in a hand-

to-hand tussle with the devil. The wife, meanwhile,
has determined on a discussion of the whole situation, xxxiv
in the hope that some understanding between them
may be reached. But his interval of cynical enjoyment and would-be detachment from emotion has left
him in no mood for passionate interviews, so he
freezes her with commonplaces and conventional
courtesies, and ' Niagara, or Vesuvius, is deferred '.
Yet he is a little uneasy under the muteness he has xxxv
again compelled, and, later, the feeling is increased
by his wife's suggestion, under cover of a game of
forfeits, that the game they play is hardly worth the
cost. The action of the next two poems maintains
the conventional level on which he has insisted. ' My
Lady ' and ' Madam ' are introduced, and their xxxvi
probing of one another's deficiencies, under cover of
appreciative comment, affords amusement to the man
who stands between them. The actors are next seen
merged in a company of persons promenading a xxxvii
garden terrace before dinner. In the harmonious and
discreet atmosphere that surrounds them all violence
seems far off and unreal. Though within sound of his
wife's voice, and, in the course of his pacings with his
partner, catching constant glimpses of his Lady, the
husband questions the existence of a problem : ' Our
tragedy,' he asks, ' is it alive or dead ? ' But the
reality of conflict and of feeling is quickly reasserted
when, in evident compunction, his friend urges him to
return to his wife. For, in one of the finest poems of xxxviii
the series, he implores his Lady to allow him to retain
in her his one spiritual anchorage ; the bond with his
wife is broken past mending, and the only remaining

choice for him is between love and vileness. The pity
of which she speaks has, he says, no place ; his wife
is like a child, who merely values a thing because it is
destroyed and is no longer to be had. To counsel him
to return to her is to drive him to evil. To his argu-
XXIX ment and his passion his Lady yields, and there follows
one golden hour of moonlight and of song in which at
last his ' bride of every sense ' seems found. Once
more his spirit is attuned to harmonies of earth and
air, and the pair stand half-dreaming beside a rippling
brook. They are in shadow when a man and woman
appear. Intruders ! who are they ? he asks, little
thinking what the answer is to be. ' The woman bears
my name and honour. Their hands touch ! ' Head-
long, all the old riot and confusion have returned ; in
XL a frenzy of feeling the husband is once more helplessly
adrift.

Peace is not to be attained by recourse to one
' inflammable to love as fire to wood ', yet his new
ecstasy is paralysed by fear that his old love is vital
still. The ground rocks under his feet ; he can be
certain of nothing—only he recognizes that the
episode with ' My Lady ' has brought no solution, and
XLI indirectly half perceives his wife's worth through the
eyes of her lover. At any rate, some attempt at
reconciliation is imperative ; beyond that he cannot
XLII see, but so far he is determined. The attempt is made,
but, unblest by love, their kisses drive them farther
XLIII apart. And in the cruel east wind of the next morning
he wanders on the seashore, imagining the meeting-
ground of wind and wave as the burial-place of love
defiled. Where or whose the fault he cannot tell, but

the evil he so dreaded has come upon him. His
bitterness has gone, but he is linked to his wife
henceforth by pity, not by love. He does his xliv
best to hide the change, but she perceives it and
will not rest content. The price of love she feels
has been paid, and she has not insight enough
to find the key to a new and deeper estrangement.
To her mind the sole explanation of her husband's
coldness lies in the existence of her rival ; he gathers xlv
a rose, and she asks him for it to grind it under foot,
convinced that it is in some way associated with his
forbidden love. And so the days go on, until at last
the awful silence is broken by an unexpected incident.
Unable one morning to find his wife, he goes half- xlvi
involuntarily to seek her in the copse which was the
scene of their courtship. He finds her there with her
lover and, going forward, offers her his arm, ignoring
the presence of a third. She accepts it without em-
barrassment, and her lover passes shadow-like and
unnoticed from their view. He feels that his wife is
on the brink of explanatory speech, and, before the
words can be framed, he declares his full confidence
in her. The storm and stress of their conflict is over,
and for a moment at least their lives are irradiated xlvii
by an afterglow of their passion. While the swallows
are gathering in the evening air, they stand together
surrounded by an atmosphere of gentleness and peace.
The husband is able at last to speak with honesty and
openness ; all that is to be said they say. But, alas
for woman's nature ! his wife cannot perceive his xlviii
meaning ; her judgement and her sensations are too
closely intertwined, and, when he introduces his

F

Lady's name, she is deaf to all else. She breaks away
from him, fixed in her idea that she must set him free
to seek her rival. Argument is useless, but none the
iess he follows and finds her on the seashore. She
XLIX takes his hand and seems amenable to his control,
happy too in his solicitude, though less vital than her
wont. Some change has come upon her. Midnight
brings the clue. She calls her husband and asks for
his embrace. She has taken poison.

Meredith's achievement in *Modern Love* lies, as
I have said, in the fact that he has been able to exalt
the situations just described to high tragedy. For,
though the philosophy and the workmanship of the
poem are worthy of his maturity, the underlying
story is inadequate. Clearly the author himself was
conscious in later life of that inadequacy ; for he
prefaced the second edition of *Modern Love* with
a poem stressing the spiritual and immaterial issues,
and at the same time (in 1892) added to the volume
The Sage Enamoured and the Honest Lady, which is a far
more subtle testing of characters in a triangular relation.
Towards its close, too, *Modern Love* more and more
escapes from the bounds of its actual story to comments
and conditions greater than attach to the given
circumstances. In the last ten divisions of the poem
the spiritual atmosphere grows steadily more exalted,
the language of metaphor rising in beauty and power,
till the forty-seventh section—which forms at once the
resting-place and the bridge between the passion and
the pitifulness—has a pellucid reflectiveness :

> We saw the swallows gathering in the sky,
> And in the osier-isle we heard them noise.

We had not to look back on summer joys,
Or forward to a summer of bright dye :
But in the largeness of the evening earth
Our spirits grew as we went side by side.
The hour became her husband and my bride.
Love that had robbed us so, thus blessed our dearth !
The pilgrims of the year waxed very loud
In multitudinous chatterings, as the flood
Full brown came from the West, and like pale blood
Expanded to the upper crimson cloud.
Love, that had robbed us of immortal things,
This little moment mercifully gave,
Where I have seen across the twilight wave
The swan sail with her young beneath her wings.

The final poem of the series culminates in a superb
image of conflicting majesty and futility in human
endeavour, and the crown is set upon a poet's vision
of mortality :

Thus piteously Love closed what he begat :
The union of this ever-diverse pair !
These two were rapid falcons in a snare,
Condemned to do the flitting of the bat.
Lovers beneath the singing sky of May,
They wandered once ; clear as the dew on flowers :
But they fed not on the advancing hours :
Their hearts held cravings for the buried day.
Then each applied to each that fatal knife,
Deep questioning, which probes to endless dole.
Ah, what a dusty answer gets the soul
When hot for certainties in this our life !—
In tragic hints here see what evermore
Moves dark as yonder midnight ocean's force,
Thundering like ramping hosts of warrior horse
To throw that faint thin line upon the shore !

F 2

CHAPTER V

POEMS OF THE ENGLISH ROADSIDE
AND SANDRA BELLONI

ON the 3rd May 1862 *Modern Love and Poems of the English Roadside* appeared. A month later George Meredith, writing to Frederick Maxse for his opinion of the volume, said, ' I saw Robert Browning the other day and he expressed himself as " astounded at the originality, delighted with the naturalness and beauty " ' ; and the same letter adds ' I shall send you the *Cornhill Magazine* next month, Adam Bede has a new work in it. I understand they have given her an enormous sum—£8,000 or more ! she retaining copyright—Bon Dieu ! will aught like this ever happen to me ? ' [1] The possibility, not indeed of thousands of pounds, but of some pecuniary reward for the work he most wanted to do—the writing of poetry—may well have seemed to Meredith to be in sight at this moment ; for, on the day before publication, *Modern Love and Poems of the English Roadside* had been subscribed ' wonderfully well '.[2]

Not only Meredith's hope for this volume of 1862, but much of his general attitude towards the writing of poetry is to be learned from a letter of his written to Augustus Jessopp in 1861 [3] ; ' As for my love of the Muse,' Meredith then wrote, ' I really think that is earnest enough. I have all my life done battle on her

[1] *Letters of George Meredith*, vol. i, p. 73.
[2] *Ibid.*, vol. i, p. 69.   [3] *Ibid.*, vol. i, p. 45.

behalf, and should, at one time, have felt no blessing to be equal to the liberty to serve her. Praise rings strangely in my ears. I have been virtually propelled into a practical turn by lack of encouragement from any other save practical work. I have no doubt it has done me good, though the pleasure your letter gives me, and let me say also the impetus, is a proof I should have flourished under a less rigorous system. If you do me the favour to look at *Once a Week* during the next two months you will see some poems of mine that are of another cast. The " Cassandra ", you will see, is as severe in rhythm as you could wish. But one result of my hard education since the publica- tion of my boy's book in '51 has been that I rarely write save from the suggestion of something actually observed . . . My Juggling Beggars, &c., I have met on the road, and have idealized but slightly. I desire to strike the poetic spark out of absolute human clay. And in doing so I have the fancy that I do solid work —better than a carol in mid air. Note " The Old Chartist " and the " Patriot Engineer ". They may not please you, but I think you will admit that they have a truth condensed in them. They are flints, perhaps, and not flowers. Well, I think of publishing a volume of Poems in the beginning of '62, and I will bring as many flowers to it as I can.'

Actually, when it came, the volume of 3rd May 1862 contained, besides *Modern Love*, twenty-two other poems.[1] *Modern Love* and the *Ode to the Spirit*

[1] *Grandfather Bridgeman, The Meeting, Juggling Jerry, The Old Chartist, The Beggar's Soliloquy, The Patriot Engineer, Cassandra, The Young Usurper, Margaret's Bridal Eve, Marian, The Head of Bran, The Morning Twilight, Autumn Even-Song, Unknown*

of Earth in Autumn are so rich in content that they have tended to dwarf the rest of this volume. Yet young readers of to-day will find in a number of the shorter poems, such as *The Old Chartist* and *Juggling Jerry*, the whole of an atmosphere and something of a style which hitherto they may have imagined to be the creation of a present-day poet. *Juggling Jerry* particularly, in its impetus of speech and colour of imagery—clear, almost heraldic, colour of gypsy caravans—bears to Mr. Masefield's *King Cole* a relationship that is singularly close. The *Ode to the Spirit of Earth in Autumn* revealed Meredith of the great stature—the poet-thinker—who was to ' extend the world at wings and dome, more spacious, making more our home ',[1] and to give the word Earth, for mankind ever afterwards, a new content.

The week which bestowed on English readers *Poems of the English Roadside* was a week of the loveliest English weather. On that 5th of May George Meredith wrote to his friend William Hardman, ' Oh, what a glorious day ! I have done lots of *Emilia*. The gorse is all ablaze, the meadows are glorious green, humming all day ; nightingales throng.' Many nights, as well as long days, of tramping the country round Copsham, had gone to the making of the Roadside Poems, yet surely it is to ' Frost on the May Night ' in *Sandra Belloni*[2] that this phrase, ' nightingales throng ', sets the mind winging.

Fair Faces, Phantasy, Shemselnihar, A Roar through the Tall Twin Elm Trees, When I would image, I Chafe at Darkness, By the Rosanna, Ode to the Spirit of Earth in Autumn, and *The Doe ; A Fragment.*   [1] *The Lark Ascending.*

[2] Originally *Emilia in England.*

Lucy Feverel has been spoken of as an ' early Victorian heroine '. That description is inadequate, but the measure of truth in it may be found in studying Lucy's successor. In Emilia, Meredith has given us his greatest of soul. Close to nature, elemental—at first a force rather than a character—to give a picture of Emilia in any way complete would be to rewrite her story ; she can only be revealed in her effect on her companions. In touch with passion and poetry at their source, she can only make them consciously her own and exercise them on the circumstances of life when she has seen herself for a time in horrible isolation from them. Her difficulties are the opposite of Wilfrid's, who can only acquire loyalty and oneness of feeling by conscious effort and sacrifice. Capacity to concentrate the whole of her physical and mental vigour on a single emotion is Emilia's from the outset. She possesses the first essential for artistic achievement, wholeheartedness. Knowing nothing of sheltered harbours or dallying rivulets, she is in midstream in hurricane as in sunlight.

But has she vision to control such force ? At the opening of the tale we are shown Emilia without self-control. The first great scene of the story—the homeward walk when Wilfrid has rescued her from a riot at a village festivity—shows Emilia lacking in perception. Through filmy summer rain, the pair hurry across a common away from the disturbance, and Emilia simply assumes the matching of Wilfrid's feelings with her own. They run, she with bowed head, and Wilfrid still holding the hand he grasped to pull her from under the tent. In order to get her

away, he has had to confess that he was the anony-
mous donor of her ruined harp, and to promise her
another. But, when at some distance from the fray
he finds that Emilia is in tears, Wilfrid proposes
leaving her at a cottage while he returns for what
remains of the instrument ; for, after all, he thinks,
it may be possible to mend it. But that is not,
Emilia says, what she is crying about. She is quite
willing to leave the harp now. Wilfrid must not
return to the tent without her ; where he goes she
must go too. Let them sit for awhile on a dry log
she sees there beneath a flowering may-bush. Marked
change has come over Emilia, her speaking voice
vibrates now with a singing richness. ' How brave
you are ! ' she presently exclaims, and all Wilfrid's
efforts to persuade her that there has been no danger
for him in the tent prove unavailing. He falls back
on the maxim that the right place for girls is at home.
' " I should like to be always where . . ." Her voice
flowed on with singular gravity to that stop.' Is it
possible she can have been going to say, ' like always
to be where he, Wilfrid, was ' ? He puts the question
more from curiosity than from anything else, for his
emotions are languid. ' To her soft " Yes " he continued briskly, and in the style of condescending
fellowship, " Of course we're not going to part."
" I wonder," said Emilia. There she sat, evidently
sounding right through the future with her young
brain to hear what Destiny might have to say.'
Touched, but conscious that he has now heard more
than he is justified in hearing, Wilfrid makes another
effort to hold to commonplaces. Accepting for the

moment Emilia's exaggerated notion of the fight in the booth, he reminds her that any honours there may have been in her rescue he shares with Captain Gambier. ' I did not see him', says Emilia.

It is, of course, Wilfrid's susceptibility to beauty, such as the beauty of Emilia's character, in combination with his want of endurance and unification of feeling, that marks him out as ' the Philosopher's prey '. None the less it is Emilia's want of insight that pushes Wilfrid, in this first love-scene between them, beyond his capacity.

Change in Emilia—the development of her that Meredith is concerned with—commences at her interview with Wilfrid's father in his office. There we witness the first conscious conflict with her instinctive actions. Compelled, as means to her end, to try to conceive the character of the man she is speaking to, to envisage his mental standpoint, consciousness of this necessity marks the beginning of a new stage in her growth. In that great scene, with its masterly study of Mr. Pole's nervous collapse, Emilia's temperamental mingling of childishness and power, of obtuseness and sensitiveness, finds full expression. She has gone up to town, to Mr. Pole's office, to plead for Wilfrid's, now avowed, love for her. Mr. Pole supposes that she has come as his daughters' emissary to persuade him to consult a doctor. The result is a heightening of the deep tragedy of the situation, by a humorous confusion, of the broad, almost Shakespearian, sort Meredith delights in. Emilia is so different from woman as Mr. Pole has known her that he finds her incalculable, and himself alternately beguiled and enraged by her words. Her passion is intense ; and she thinks in images that work as acid on his sensitized physical condition—prospect of division from Wilfrid is, she says, frost in her bones ; her heart jerks, each time it beats, as though dragging her body out of the grave ; if Mr. Pole slaughters her love and his son's, what mercy, what pity, in the whole universe can sufferings of his own anywhere find ? The boon Emilia is demanding is now out of Mr. Pole's power to grant. Yet the force of her speech so fastens upon him that he can loose himself from it only by a crying out of the secret he has guarded with his life. Meanwhile, a few chapters earlier, in the great love-scene between Wilfrid and Emilia, Emilia's high spiritual destiny has been indicated. Worthy to rank with the lyric loves of Richard Feverel and Lucy, rapturous as those earliest hours, ' By Wilming Weir ' is permeated with an even more delicate beauty. Emilia and Wilfrid are older in experience than Richard and Lucy ; and, though Emilia is as yet immature and uncomplex, this is due more to slow ripening of a great nature than to dainty guilelessness or ordinary simplicity, for she has known hunger and contact with evil. The feeling that possesses her as, from the darkening meadow, she watches the twisting light upon the weir is as poignant with foreboding as with ecstasy. On Richard and Lucy the moon had shone ' young as upon the lovers in Paradise ' ; now she is red-gold with the passion of centuries. Encom-passed with the falling of waters and the twirling of the moonbeams, Emilia's mind is possessed by her art. Presently, when Wilfrid arrives and entreats her, she does indeed consent to sacrifice music and Italy to love for him. Yet her personal passion already is in touch with things outside itself ; she says ' Do you know, when we were silent just now, I was thinking that water was the history of the world flowing out before me, all mixed up of kings and queens, and warriors with armour, and shouting armies; battles and numbers of mixed people ; and great red sunsets, with women kneeling under them. Do you know those long, low sunsets ? I love them. They look like blood spilt for love. The noise of the water, and the moist green smell, gave me hundreds of pictures that seemed to hug me '. Wilfrid, at the threshold only of genuine emotion, is engrossed in hoping that his courage may compass the normal human endeavour of winning and holding for his wife this girl whom he recognizes as more nearly superhuman in spirit than any he has known. Emilia, on the other hand, already has sight of a more commanding ideal. A year later she is to say ' May no dear woman I know ever marry the man she first loves '. But, till Wilfrid shall unmistakably desert her, Emilia's devotion to him will be complete. It is her author only who perceives that the gossamer hours, flying like white doves off the mounting moon at Wilming Weir, carry with them from this pair of lovers the best that is to be. As they turn homeward from the silver greensward, beneath the velvet blackness of the bank glides a swan ; and the atmosphere Meredith here renders is almost identical with that of his magical stanza XLVII of *Modern Love*.

As a milestone of Emilia's development, even more

marked than the scene in Mr. Pole's office, is the
incident when, forsaken by Wilfrid and in terror of
losing her voice, she stands before a mirror, appraising
the attractiveness of her appearance, and asking how
that may be enhanced—' The one Emilia, so unquestioning, so sure, lay dead ; and a dozen new
spirits, with but a dim likeness to her, were fighting
for possession of her frame, now occupying it alone,
now in couples ; and each casting grim reflections on
the other. Which is only a way of telling you that
the great result of mortal suffering—consciousness—
had fully set in ; to ripen ; perhaps to debase ; at any
rate, to prove her '. Meredith's philosophy probably
allows too little for the virtue and beauty of natures
who ' where no misgiving is ' rely on their unanalysed
instincts. His noble women, one and all, win to
their spiritual freedom through suffering. Emilia,
humiliated, craves to see herself of worth in other
people's eyes. The question, as Meredith sees it, is—
will she employ her merely feminine and mercantile
attributes, trade on her appearance, or will she deter-
mine to be valuable in her own eyes, mould herself from
within outwards ? It is answered in Tracy Runningbrook's letters to Wilfrid, after Emilia's illness, which
describe her as perceiving herself and her power of love
as materials to be moulded to beauty, instruments
to be harmonized. This perception, with the con-
trolling and garnering of instinctive emotion it implies,
is the key of Emilia's development, sustained till the
close of *Vittoria*, where Meredith can say of his heroine,
' Rarely has a soul been so subjected by its own force.
She certainly had the image of God in her mind.'

Though not published till 1864 the writing of
Sandra Belloni (originally *Emilia in England*) had
occupied much of Meredith's three previous years.
As early as the 17th May 1861 he had written to
Janet Ross that the most advanced of the works he
had then in hand was ' Emilia Belloni '.[1] Had we no
other testimony than this book to the reviving of
Meredith's spirits through 1862 and 1863 that would be
sufficient. It has intensity enough to fuse the leading
characteristics of Meredith's thought, and to show us
the springs of many of his convictions at their source.
Emilia is an unveiling of an ideal. All the persons
she directly touches—Tracy Runningbrook, Merthyr,
Wilfrid, Lady Charlotte, even Mr. Pole and Mr. Peri-
cles—are lit with her fire. With her as their pivot,
these characters move in the radius of their author's
genius, the circle of essential feeling where Meredith's
touch never errs. But outside that circle are a
number of characters of whom the best that can be
said is that they may not have been meant to be
inside it. The sisters Pole, despite the prolixity with
which they are analysed, belong to the same class as
the Ladies Culmer and Busshe of *The Egoist*—the
large class of Meredith's unvitalized characters who
are not individuals, but who form collectively a middle
distance between the live persons and the background.
Viewed thus, as representing the ' fine shades ', the
' nice feelings ', the Misses Pole serve the unfolding of
the tale ; none the less before Mrs. Chump offers
Emilia a sovereign for information as to who pairs
with whom, and what the sisters are meaning, the

[1] *Letters of George Meredith*, vol. i, p. 25.

reader has wearied of their manœuvres. Edward
Buxley, Sir Twickenham Pryme, Captain Gambier
and Purcell Barrett, too, are little better than lay
figures. Yet in view of the heart of the story, we may
question whether this want of vitalization has not
a use. Housemaids allege that sunshine puts their
fires out; Emilia glows among these shadows like
a star.

Meredith's avowal of ethical and philosophical
meaning in *Sandra Belloni* is explicit. The story is
an exposition of the differences between Sentiment
and Passion. He who travels to Love by the road of
Sentiment finds himself enclosed in a vacuum,
insulated from realities; caught up on to a steed
called Hippogriff, 'the foal of Fiery Circumstance out
of Sentiment'. Wilfrid Pole is the rider on Hippogriff. Emilia Belloni is carried upon True Passion
which, Meredith says, is noble strength on fire;
sane, and not, if thwarted, turning upon its
possessor; 'constantly just to itself, mind! This is
the quality of true passion. Those who make a noise
and are not thus distinguishable are on Hippogriff.'
Such frank confession of theory in this book cannot
have been very difficult to Emilia's author, who must
have been aware that he had succeeded in giving to
her and to Wilfrid vitality enough to overflow any
philosopher's formula. As opposed to Emilia, Wilfrid
may represent a sentimentalist, but the man who was
later to charge without weapons at the battle of
Novara, and willingly to suffer degradation and insult
in saving Emilia and her Italian husband from her
enemies, is sound at core; and Meredith's cogent plea

for his readers' patience with Wilfrid has been quoted already in reference to *Evan Harrington.*

Merthyr Powys is Meredith's favourite among his Welshmen ; in praise of Merthyr little further needs to be said. His solicitude for Emilia gives us some of the loveliest passages of the book. He is, he asserts, never at a loss in his understanding of Cymric or Italian nature ; and Emilia, he boasts to his sister Georgiana, as well as being Italian, is, on her mother's side, Welsh. Emilia says to Georgiana, whose standards of behaviour she often fails to satisfy, ' Merthyr *waits* for me,' adding in reply to Georgiana's question as to why she did not sooner break her foolish promise to Wilfrid—' I could not *see through it* till now.' And in these sentences Merthyr's bearing throughout *Sandra Belloni* and *Vittoria* is summarized. In his protracted task of wooing Emilia back to living and self-confidence, after her first recovery from physical starvation, his imaginative tenderness is unfailing. He flatters her, accompanies her to balls, designs her dresses, even, to wake her pride. But these are merely his initial services ; his inestimable gift to Emilia's need is his refusal to offer his love to any but her whole nature.

In Tracy Runningbrook Meredith has allowed himself a luxury. Having created Emilia, he frees himself of the limitations of prose by handing description of her, after her illness, to a poet. Invited by Merthyr Powys to constitute himself Emilia's mentor and daily companion, when she is slowly recovering, Tracy writes from Monmouth a series of letters about her to Wilfrid—letters conveying the shaping and emerging of the loveliness that was instinct in her personality. Tracy's sensitiveness, too, is medium for the culminating scene of the story—scene that muted the nightingales even—" Frost on the Night in May ". Meredith, in these years, had seen a good deal of Swinburne ; and in the red-headed Tracy Runningbrook [1] he has embodied the essential of one who appeared to the admirers among his contemporaries as poetry incarnate.

[1] The very name—Runningbrook—suggests a play on the name Swinburne.

CHAPTER VI

MARRIAGE
RHODA FLEMING, 1864–1865

THE first letter we possess of Meredith's concerning a Vulliamy family is of the 28th October 1863.[1] An old Mr. Vulliamy, father of three sons and four daughters, had come from Normandy to settle in England some seven years earlier; and for five of those years had been living at Mickleham near Dorking. His three sons remained in business in France, and his eldest daughter was married there; but with him in his Surrey home were the three younger girls—Betty, Kitty, and Marie. By the late spring of 1864 Meredith's special interest in Miss Marie is evident; and on the 29th May he is writing to William Hardman requesting Hardman to come down immediately to Mickleham to assure Marie's father in regard to the moral character and sufficient pecuniary resources of her suitor George Meredith. By the end of that August Meredith is living beside the Vulliamys at Mickleham, and in the following month, September of 1864, he and Marie Vulliamy are married.

Early in October they are honeymooning in Frederick Maxse's house on Southampton Water; Meredith reports himself to be radiantly happy and working mightily, and speaks in particular of a one-volume novel—'plain', 'right excellent story',[2] for next January publication, *Rhoda Fleming* by name.

[1] *Letters of George Meredith*, vol. i, p. 123.
[2] *Ibid.*, vol. i, pp. 158–62.

G

On the 29th May to Hardman,[1] and on the 6th June
to Frederick Maxse,[2] Meredith had told of his determination to change his method of writing—' to enter
life with my people—to make money '—and of this
resolution *Rhoda Fleming, A Plain Story*, was the
firstfruit.   In this book certainly Meredith has
proved, past all dispute, his mastery of the simplest
chords of human emotion, his ability to reveal tragic
depths in unsophisticated persons.   Such chapters as
' Dahlia's Frenzy ' and ' When the Night is Darkest '
are almost perfect in poignancy and directness of
expression.   Rhoda and Dahlia Fleming are daughters
of a Kentish working farmer, and the opening of the
tale is concerned with their mother's devotion to her
garden, and the girls' life on the farm.   Reduced to
its framework, the story is an account of Dahlia's
visit to London, her seduction and desertion there by
a nephew of the squire of her village, and Rhoda's
consequent suffering.   A good deal is recounted of
Edward Blancove—Dahlia's lover—and of his cousin
Algernon, and their circles.   But, intentionally or not,
these upper-class persons have no vitality comparable
with the Flemings ; interest is centred in Dahlia and
Rhoda throughout.

Though Rhoda gives title to the story, Dahlia's
tragedy is supreme in it.   Near the beginning Dahlia's
character is revealed to us in her letters.   The first
of these is to Edward Blancove, when, at eleven
o'clock one night, unexpectedly finding Rhoda asleep
in her bed at her London lodgings, she has dismissed

[1] *Letters of George Meredith*, vol. i, p. 145.
[2] *Ibid.*, vol. i, p. 150.

her lover from her window, without explanation.
The letter is delivered to Edward at his Inn chambers
next morning ; and what it reveals of the intensity
of Dahlia's normal, sisterly love signifies the potency
of her passion for Edward. The statements of the
letter appear unquestionable—she has wept through
the whole of the night, she moves this morning like
a ghost, her existence is unreal till she has knowledge
of Edward's forgiveness—but it is the simple, background fact Dahlia recounts that gives these assur-
ances their poignancy : ' In my bed there lay my
sister, and I could not leave her, *I love her so.* I could
not have got downstairs after seeing her there ; I had
to say that cold word and shut the window.' The
second of Dahlia's letters is written to Rhoda some
months later, when Rhoda has returned to the farm.
Dahlia writes that she is leaving England that very
day, and continues, ' I must not love you too much,
for I have all my love to give to my Edward, my own
now, and I am his trustingly for ever. But he will let
me give you some of it—and Rhoda is never jealous.
She shall have a great deal. Only I am frightened
when I think how *immense* my love is for him ; so
that anything—everything he thinks right is right
to me. I am not afraid to think so. . . . I am like
drowned to everybody but one. We are looking at
the sea. In half an hour I shall have forgotten the
tread of English earth. I do not know that I breathe.
All I know is a fear that I am flying and my strength
will not continue. That is when I am not touching
his hand. There is France opposite. I shut my eyes
and see the whole country but it is like what I feel

for Edward—all in dark moonlight. Oh! I trust him
so! I bleed for him. I could *make* all my veins bleed
out at a sad thought about him. And from France to
Switzerland and Italy. The sea sparkles just as if it
said " Come to the sun " : and I am going. . . . Here
is Edward. He says I *may* send his *love* to you.
Address : Mrs. Edward Ayrton, Poste Restante,
Lausanne, Switzerland. P.S.—Lausanne is where—
but another time, and I will always tell you the
history of the places to instruct you, poor heart in dull
England. Adieu! Good-bye, and God bless my
innocent at home, my dear sister. I love her. I never
can forget her. The day is so lovely. It seems on
purpose for us. Be sure you write on thin paper to
Lausanne. It is on a blue lake : you see snow
mountains, and now there is a bell ringing—kisses
from me! we start. I must sign.—Dahlia.' It is
almost impossible, in spite of Edward Blancove's dis-
loyalty and all the machinations of Mrs. Lovell, to
think of Dahlia as ever being argued, or arguing
herself, into thought of marriage with any one but
Edward. But one of the most masterly traits of the
whole book is the use to which Meredith put his
experience of physical illness, in Dahlia's history.
Such mental energy as remains to her, after her fever,
spends itself in the mere revival of memory ; she
has no surplus strength to meet and refute arguments.
Momentarily she can flame with passion ; but usually
she is frozen or plastic in her sister's hands. Rhoda
has been always the more active in character ; after
the catastrophe it is she who determines all actions.
Sedgett, too, villain as he is, stands to Rhoda and her

father, and is of course intended to stand, for a principle.

It has been remarked more than once that George Meredith's novels owe a good deal to Richardson's. That remark, however, has not been explained or expanded, and, though Sir Charles Grandison is recalled by name in *The Ordeal of Richard Feverel*, it is in no very serious connexion. The immense differences between the novels of Richardson and of Meredith need not be dwelt on here, nor is it necessary to emphasize distinctions between English public opinion in 1748 and 1864. Yet Richardson's women are more created from within outward than are the women of any other writer of his day ; at any rate Richardson had the temerity to question then prevailing conceptions of the feminine sex and at least to attempt an answer to Mowbray's astonished outcry at Lovelace's grief over Clarissa, ' She was but a woman, and what was there in one woman more than another ? ' *Clarissa*, spite of its superficial differences, and its sermonizing, has much in common with *Rhoda Fleming*. Lovelace's anguish, when he realizes that Clarissa's soul has escaped his reach, that it is ' out of his power anyway in the world to be even with her ', is closely parallel with Edward's. Lovelace writes to a friend of Clarissa, who is dying, and refuses to see him or consider his offers of marriage, ' Has not her triumph over me, from first to last, been infinitely greater than her sufferings from me ? Would the sacred regard I have for her purity, even for her *personal* as well as *intellectual* purity, permit, I could prove this as clear as the sun. Hence it is that I admire her more than ever, and that my love for her is less personal, as I may say more *intellectual* than ever I thought it could be to a woman.' Meredith tells us of Edward, when, after Dahlia's recovery from attempted suicide, he is entreating her to marry him, ' He had three interviews with Dahlia ; he wrote to her as many times. There was but one answer for him ; and when he ceased to charge her with unforgivingness, he came to the strange conclusion that beyond our calling a woman a Saint for rhetorical purposes, and esteeming her as one for pictorial, it is indeed possible both to think her saintly and to have the sentiments inspired by the over-earthly in her presence.' Richardson put into the scale with his heroine a heavy makeweight of circumstances— abduction, rank, frailty of physique—yet that hardly lessens his achievement in making Clarissa, disowned and cast out by her family and dying unmarried, accepted by his time as spiritually triumphant. In *Rhoda Fleming* the climax is similar ; though Dahlia's final feeling for her lover is much more delicate than Clarissa's. Dahlia does not proffer Christian charity and prayers for Edward's amendment ; all that she has is Edward's. But her personality has been reft of capacity for joy. In Clarissa's story, death was the culminating touch ; tragedy could no farther go. In Dahlia's, death would have been inadequate, an evasion of tragedy. Her story, more delicate, more poignant, demands death in life—burying alive—as its end ; ' She lived seven years her sister's housemate, nurse of the growing swarm. She had gone through fire, as few women have done in like manner, to leave their hearts among the ashes ; but with that human heart she left regrets behind her. The soul filled its place. It shone in her eyes and in her work, a lamp in her little neighbourhood ; and not less a lamp of cheerful beams for one day being as another to her. When she died she relinquished nothing. Others knew the loss.'

The impassive countryman, Farmer Fleming, normally incapable of passion and not responsive to any ordinary stimulus, is in one sense the greatest creation of the book. In his wife's lifetime he was shown capable of the small degree of feeling requisite for nursing a grievance. He considered his wife's gardening an extravagance, and resented bitterly her suggestion that he should relinquish the farm, on which he was losing money, to join her in converting her flourishing flower-garden into a commercial undertaking. But his speechlessness was such that, except in regard to this practical change, his wife managed him to her end, and died unaware of his resentment. Yet from the moment Dahlia's letter arrives, announcing her marriage but giving no surname, he is inexorable. He is shown to us only in isolated and occasional acts ; but his impact is constantly felt. Instinct and tradition of generations are operating by him. The ' respectability ' Dahlia has forfeited, and which is miraculously offered to her again, is a matter as little to be escaped as the forces of nature. He epitomizes the awfulness of stupidity, of convictions not amenable to reasoning. But he is a figure none the less heroic in scale because pitiless—a figure representing much more than himself, and the very keynote of the tragedy. For Meredith's insight makes clear to us here, as of Nataly in *One of Our Conquerors*, that the force Dahlia and Nataly oppose has gathered through ages, and, though it find earliest expression in criticism by others, has its final stronghold in instincts of the rebels themselves. The colossal proportions of this force can, in modern life, be best represented in dramas set among primitive persons. A similar force, operating in higher social circles, is so differentiated as to produce its impression only fragmentarily. And here, probably, we have the reason why *One of Our Conquerors*, in spite of its greater subtlety, is less overpowering than *Rhoda Fleming* in tragic effect.

CHAPTER VII

1864–1871; *VITTORIA*; INTERNATIONAL AFFAIRS; *HARRY RICHMOND*

'MY "plain story" is first to right me and then the three-volumer will play trumpets.'[1] Meredith was heading his letters still from Frederick Maxse's house, and the three-volumer was *Vittoria*. *Emilia in England (Sandra Belloni)* early in 1864 had proved a considerable success, and in May of that year Meredith had written to William Hardman, ' I think I shall have to go to Italy, for every one says *Emilia in Italy*[2] should be forthcoming as speedily as may be.'[3] A good deal too is said by him in letters to friends at this time about the differences they were to find between the stories of Emilia in England and Emilia in Italy ; in Italy, he said, his heroine moved adventurously, undogged by philosopher or analyst, on a field of plain issues and activities. Through the autumn and winter of 1864 Meredith's interest in what was then taking place in Italy was manifestly growing. His happy marriage, however, had intervened, and William Maxse Meredith, his son by this marriage, was in the world, before, in the late autumn of 1865, *Vittoria* was completed. Warmly approved by G. H. Lewes, at that time editor of the *Fortnightly Review*, it began to appear in that review

[1] *Letters of George Meredith*, vol. i, p. 162.
[2] Afterwards named *Vittoria*.
[3] *Letters of George Meredith*, vol. i, p. 141.

in February of 1866 ; and by July of 1866 Meredith
had been sent to the seat of war in Italy as correspondent to the *Morning Post*. Except for a three-
weeks' return to England at the end of July, he was
in Italy through that autumn and into the winter.
Such matter of the fighting between Italy and
Austria as he found time to report is collected now in
Correspondence from the Seat of War in Italy in the
Memorial Edition of Meredith's works.

That *Vittoria* was dear to its writer's heart is
evidenced by a number of his letters in 1866 and the
early spring of 1867, and by two letters to Swinburne
in particular. In the first of these Meredith writes of
his uplifting of heart at Swinburne's praise, because
Vittoria's publishers and others have been informing
him that the book is not liked ; [1] and in the second
letter, on the 2nd March 1867, the disappointed author
pours out, to the understanding writer of ' A Song of
Italy ' and ' The Halt before Rome ', the aims he had
had in this novel. ' My object,' he says, ' was not
to write the Epic of the Revolt—for that the time is
yet too new ; but to represent the revolt itself, with
the passions animating both sides, the revival of the
fervid Italian blood ; and the character of the people :
Luigi Saracco, Barto Rizzo, &c. Agostino Balderini
is purposely made sententious and humorously
conscious of it : Carlo Ammiani is the personification
of the youth of Italy of the nobler sort. Laura Piaveni
and Violetta d'Isorella are existing contrasts. I am
afraid it must be true that the style is stiff ; but a
less condensed would not have compassed the great

[1] *Letters of George Meredith*, vol. i, p. 182.

amount of matter.' Certainly, as a tale, *Vittoria* has been choked by its weight of matter. The swiftly moving story of clear incidents, promised when Emilia should be removed to Italy, is not here. The plot is ill-constructed, or rather not constructed at all. The book contains certain great narrative passages, such as the duel scene in the Stelvio Pass, and some first-rate descriptions of nature ; but it is not successful as a novel. It is a poet's account of historical incidents of which he had intimate knowledge. The opening chapter gives us Emilia of *Sandra Belloni*, renamed now Vittoria, on a mountain-top in conclave with half a dozen leaders of the Italian Independence movement and their chief Mazzini. She is presented here as the Emilia we have known, developed to a trusted patriot, and being commissioned by Mazzini at this critical moment to give the signal for the rising of Milan. Yet within half an hour of this solemn dedication on Monte Motterone she is being so inconsequent as to leave around written messages betraying the plan of the rising. Emilia, in the youngest of *Sandra Belloni* days, could not have acted like that. She was indeed unmindful of other people's feelings in her concentration on a central emotion— Lady Charlotte's towards Wilfrid hardly had existed for her. But such error is at the opposite pole from the error at the opening of the Italian story. Just what secondary considerations the maturer Emilia might have held in mind between her exaltation on Motterone and the date of the rising in Milan, those of us who loved her as she was in England would not have ventured to assert. But to the fact that no

earthly power could cause her to be for a moment
dulled to her mission all who had earlier known her
would swear.

The life of *Vittoria* is in its noble dramatization of
certain personages and single events. Its descriptions
of Mazzini make up a portrait that has not been
rivalled by professional historians.[1] ' He was,'
Meredith says, ' a man of middle stature, thin and
even frail ; with the complexion of the student, and
the student's aspect. The attentive droop of his
shoulders and head, the straining of his buttoned coat
across his chest, the air as of one who waited and
listened, which distinguished his figure, detracted
from the promise of other than contemplative energy,
until his eyes were fairly seen and felt. That is, until
the observer became aware that those soft and large,
dark meditative eyes had taken hold of him. In them
lay no abstracted student's languor, no reflex burning
of a solitary lamp ; but a quiet, grappling force
engaged the penetrating look. Gazing upon them,
you were drawn in suddenly among the thousand
whirring wheels of a capacious and vigorous mind,
that was both reasoning and prompt, keen of intellect,
acting throughout all its machinery, and having all
under full command ; an orbed mind, supplying its
own philosophy, and arriving at the sword-stroke by
logical steps—a mind much less supple than a soldier's ;
anything but the mind of Hamlet. . . . He saw far, and
he grasped ends beyond obstacles ; he was nourished

---

[1] The Englishman who knows most of this period of Italian
history is Mr. George Trevelyan, than whom no one living is
a more whole-hearted admirer of Meredith's work.

by sovereign principles ; he despised material present
interests ; and, as I have said, he was less supple than
a soldier. If the title of idealist belonged to him, we
will not immediately decide that it was opprobrious.
The idealized conception of stern truths played about
his head certainly for those who knew and who loved
it. Such a man, perceiving a devout end to be reached,
might prove less scrupulous in his course, possibly, and
less remorseful than revolutionary Generals. His
smile was quite unclouded, and came softly as a curve
in water. It seemed to flow with, and to pass in and
out of, his thoughts—to be a part of his emotion and
his meaning when it shone transiently full. For as he
had an orbed mind, so he had an orbed nature. The
passions were absolutely in harmony with the intelligence.' And in the four closing lines that Meredith
puts into his heroine's mouth in the great scene at
La Scala he finally embodied his understanding of the
creed of Young Italy's chief :

> Our life is but a little holding, lent
> To do a mighty labour : we are one
> With heaven and the stars when it is spent
> To serve God's aim : else die we with the sun.

Yet when all is said in regard to the failure of
Vittoria as a story, we come to the clear-cut cameo
of the heroine, composed of Emilia in England and
Emilia in Italy, at the end. Vittoria searching the
mountains with Merthyr, bringing all her force to
hold herself in poise between the past and the future, is
hardly to be spoken of in words other than Meredith's.
We are here face to face with the commanding ideal,
the high destiny foreshadowed in *Sandra Belloni.*

Meredith set out to balance and combine an idealist and an artist, and to perfect them both in a woman. Vittoria, pursuing a political ideal, has not had to turn away from her art or her personal relations. The ideal, high but not remote, has embraced every part of her nature. Her perfect response to every daily demand has now its perfect reward. She has the instinct of surrender, and so she cannot be robbed. Merthyr and she travel the mountains looking for her husband, and they are likelier to find him dead than alive : ' Vittoria read the faces of the mornings as human creatures have tried to gather the sum of their destinies off changing surfaces—fair not meaning fair, nor black black, but either the mask upon the secret of God's terrible will ; and to learn it and submit, was the spiritual burden of her motherhood, that the child leaping with her heart might live. Not to hope blindly, in the exceeding anxiousness of her passionate love, nor blindly to fear ; not to let her soul fly out among the twisting chances ; not to sap her great maternal duty by affecting false stoical serenity—to nurse her soul's strength, and suckle her womanly weakness with the tears which are poison when repressed ; to be at peace with a disastrous world for the sake of the dependent life unborn ; by such pure efforts she clung to God. Soft dreams of sacred nuptial tenderness, tragic images, wild pity, were like phantoms encircling her, plucking at her as she went ; but they were beneath her feet, and she kept them from lodging between her breasts. The thought that her husband, though he should have perished, was not a life lost if their child lived, sustained her powerfully.

It seemed to whisper at times almost, as it were Carlo's ghost breathing in her ears: "On thee!" On her the further duty devolved ; and she trod down hope, lest it should build her up and bring a shock to surprise her fortitude : she put back alarm. The mountains and the valleys scarce had names for her understanding ; they were but a scene where the will of her Maker was at work. Rarely has a soul been so subjected by its own force. She certainly had the image of God in her mind.' ' Not to let her soul fly out among the twisting chances '—to Meredith that achievement is the end and aim of this earth's discipline. Not to lose the capacities for desire and aspiration, but to control and subdue them to working within our allotment, instead of being dragged at their heels—such is his reading of life, though it involved for him as for Vittoria disburdening of Hope as well as of Fear.

Among the most interesting of George Meredith's letters are those of 1870 and 1871 regarding the outbreak of the Franco-Prussian War. They are quoted at some length here because of their bearing on the cataclysm of our own time. On the 25th July 1870 he writes to John Morley : ' The war of '70 is the direct issue of '66. Just as we abused the Prussians then we howl at the French now, but the tremendous armaments on both sides were meant for this duel, and it mattered very little what was the pretext for the outbreak. Surely it is a case of Arcades Ambo. The French felt themselves perpetually menaced by distended Prussia, irritated by her tone, even alarmed by the rumour and dread of projects, the existence of which her antecedents might seem to warrant. At any rate it was a fight to come on ; and here we have it ; and if we are energetic and wise it may be the last of the great fights of Europe. The two foremost States in war and intellect may well be committed to cut the bloody tangle. I feel deeply for the Germans ; I quite understand the ardour of the French. I think their cause, from their point of view, thoroughly good, and not likely to succeed.' [1] In October of that year, 1870, to his son Arthur, then at school in Stuttgart, he wrote, ' Tell Professor Zeller, with my compliments, that if there is a fund for the wounded soldiers in Stuttgart I shall be glad if he will put down my name for the subscription of £1. I cannot afford more just now. The French peasantry around Sedan claim everything of us that we can give. They are barely held up in life by the bread we are able to furnish ; and a third of France will be demanding succour in the winter. Horrible to think of !—but do not let compassion or personal sympathy make your judgement swerve. This war is chargeable upon France, and the Emperor is the Knave of the pack. Two generations of Frenchmen have been reared on the traditions of Napoleonism, and these meant the infliction of wrongs and outrages on other nations for the glory and increase of their own. They elected a Napoleon for chief because of his name, and in spite of his known character. It is said the French peasantry did not want war ; that their ignorance offended in electing this man ; but who can deny that it was the Napoleonic prestige which gave him his

---

[1] *Letters of George Meredith,* vol. i, pp. 210–11.

first step to the throne by overwhelming votes ? This man was the expression of their ignorance, or folly, or vanity ; he appealed to the Napoleonism in them, and had a prompt response. A more ignoble spectacle than the recriminations of Emperor and people upon one another as to the origin of the war, after defeat, history does not show. The Germans, on the con-trary, reap the reward of a persistently honourable career in civic virtue. Consider what the meaning of civic virtue may be. It comprises a multitude of other virtues. As to German boasting, why, the English also are great boasters. See the best in those about you. I say this, and I admire and respect the Germans, and God knows my heart bleeds for the French. But my aim, and I trust it will be yours, is never to take counsel of my sensations, but of my intelligence. I let the former have free play, but deny them the right to bring me to a decision. You are younger, have a harder task in doing that ; you have indeed a task in discerning the difference between what your senses suggest and what your mind. How-ever, try not to be let into some degree of injustice to your host, the German people, out of pity for France. . . . Captain Maxse is out and out French ; Mr. Morison intensely German ; Mr. Morley and I do our utmost to preserve an even balance. There is talk of an armistice, but Paris must fall before the French will seriously treat for peace. Count Bismarck gives audience to-day to that deleterious little Frenchman Thiers, who has been poisoning his countrymen for half a century, and now runs from Court to Court, from minister to minister, to get help to undo his own direct work. Count Bismarck will be amused, for he has a keen appreciation of comedy. Philosophers would laugh aloud at the exhibition of the author of *The Consulate and the Empire* in the camp at Versailles. Modern France has been nourished on this lying book.'[1] George Meredith's fairness of mind in these letters is the more valuable and remarkable from the fact that he was at this time in great perturbation of mind about his wife's three brothers, who owned spinning-mills and lived, at Nonancourt on the Avre. On the day he was writing the above-quoted letter to Arthur Meredith, the Germans were coming upon Dreux; two months later, 26 December 1870, they were at Nonancourt, and Henri Poussielque, husband of Mrs. Meredith's eldest sister, was in the thick of the fighting.

The *Fortnightly Review* of January 1871 contained Meredith's great *Ode to France*. Written in December 1870 when the German Army was encircling Paris, this *Ode* has the ring of an adamantine reality that our day has experienced :

> We look for her that sunlike stood
> Upon the forehead of our day,
> An orb of nations, radiating food
> For body and for mind alway.
> Where is the Shape of glad array ;
> The nervous hands, the front of steel,
> The clarion tongue ? Where is the bold, proud face ?
> *We see a vacant place ;*
> *We hear an iron heel.*

From this opening, to its closing lines, the poem

---

[1] *Letters of George Meredith*, vol. i, pp. 213–14.

is a high tribute to France. But those closing lines :

> Soaring France !
> How is Humanity on trial in thee :
> How mayst thou gather humankind in fee :
> Now prove that Reason is a quenchless scroll ;
> Make of calamity thine aureole,
> And bleeding, head us through the troubles of the sea ;

need as their gloss Meredith's words written to Frederick Maxse on the 27th February 1871 :

'Things are saddening enough in France. But I do not remember the gloomy forecasts following the wars of Napoleon I. The Germans have retaliated in coin. They too must pay for it. These developments only prove that our speculations were more advanced than realities. Through such a course of teaching men must go. Can you pretend to believe that France was not in need of the bitterest of lessons ? Her philosophers said one thing, but military glory stuck to the passions of her people. And many of her philosophers allowed themselves to be hoodwinked by the idea that France should be dominant " for the good of mankind ", instead of seeking to make her dominant by virtue and a bright example. She trusted to the sword without even testing her steel. She is down. I grieve for her ; I detest the severities practised upon her. But I cannot forget that she appealed to the *droit de plus fort*. Nor can I forget that she has always been the perturbation of Europe. The Germans may be. That is to be seen. They at least are what they pretend to be. . . . I prefer to wait without prophesying. Let France train a virtuous democracy, and she will spring a mine in Germany amply to be revenged on the Hohenzollerns. Her cries of vengeance now are after the pattern—too shockingly similar !—of Ancient Pistol. She "eats and e'en she swears".... Confess that the French have conducted themselves like mere children throughout. The probation may accelerate their growth and bring their practice up to their best professions. The Germans have behaved as the very sternest of men, caring more for their Fatherland than for the well-being of men in the mass. I am susceptible of admiration of their sterling qualities, holding nevertheless that they will repent of the present selfish restriction of their views.—Rage at me, Fred ! It is better to bend the knee to Wisdom than march in the chorusing ranks of the partizans.—I think with pain that the Germans enter Paris this very day ! But the City is not a " holy City " for me. The astonishing delusion which makes Frenchmen think it so is one proof of rudderless brains. Morley is not " German ". He agrees with me that it would have been a silly madness to create a terrible and justly wrathful enemy for ourselves (looking to the origin of this war), on the chance of securing a frenzied, fantastical ally. So will you in time. Generous sympathies hold you spell-bound.—

Your ever loving
GEORGE MEREDITH.'

In 1870, in the ' Cornhill Magazine ', *Harry Richmond* was appearing. The reader who falls under the spell of one after another of Meredith's novels is obliged to be on his guard against naming more than one of them as the greatest. The range of characterization is so large, the inequalities within the same book are so marked, that an estimate of each, or a comparison of each with all the rest, is singularly difficult. If *Harry Richmond* might be divided into two halves, of the

first half it would be easy to say : ' Here is the greatest
of Meredith's novels.' This portion, comprising
Harry's boyhood with his grandfather and father,
his stay at the farm, journey with Kiomi, voyage with
Captain Bulstead, and travels in Germany, is among
the most remarkable feats in our literature. The first
page plunges us into the heart of the story. That
midnight tussle between the grandfather and father
for possession of the child is the most skilful of backgrounds for the kaleidoscopic fantasy of Harry's
after life. A lesser novelist might have moved Roy
Richmond and his son entertainingly enough on
a No-man's-land ; but the wonder of Meredith's
exploit is that their life appears credible woven on the
most British of backgrounds. The balance between
fantasy and sanest prose is sustained right through
the book. When Shylock's descendant walks away
with Roy Richmond, Harry is conveyed to a home-
stead pervaded with smells of butter and cheese ;
while Roy is playing jester to a German Principality,
Harry is at the most solid of schools ; Kiomi and her
parents are at the door of the stiff Beltham house, but
Kiomi is 'fresh of the East as on the morning when her
ancient people struck tents in the track of their
shadows '. And the, no small, result of this delicacy
of counterpoise is the reader's sensation that the
palaces and pageants of the sky with which the
novelist is surrounding him have their match in his
own experience ; human existence, inexhaustible,
indefinable, but in some way verifiable and familiar, is
before him.

The last half of the book does not equal the first.

Yet the last portion has much subtlety and delicacy of interest. In that, Harry Richmond, true son of his father, is in sight of his goal ; but not more than in sight of it, because he is his father's son. Persons there are in life who through impressional suscepti-bility—gift for passionate appreciation—take rank for a time with persons greatly their superior in nature ; and it is not the smallest of Harry Rich-mond's achievements that the Princess Ottilia exists for us through him. For if Ottilia is not the greatest of George Meredith's heroines, it is because the atmosphere she breathes is too rare for the normal reader. No decision against marriage with Harry Richmond is ever expressed or formulated by her ; the barrier is founded in more than difference of rank. Not to be undermined, it might have been leaped. But a giant such as Ferdinand Lassalle would have been needed for that. It was a feat ludicrously out of reach of a youth whose susceptibility had no tried courage to back it.

If any proof were needed of the fact that George Meredith's genius lies in poetic grasp rather than in analysis of minutiae, *Harry Richmond* would supply it. The range of its incident and characterization is immense. No summary, even, of these can be attempted here. One personage, however, there is in the book beside whom all others fall into obscurity. Roy Richmond is one of the very greatest, if not the greatest, of Meredith's creations. He is *the* Tragic Comedian. For, excepting the fundamentals, he possesses all the heroic qualities. His affections are strong, his tastes fine and delicate, he is fearless and

marvellously resourceful. To Squire Beltham, whose
daughter he has crazed, he appears all that is mean and
despicable ; but to his small boy, and to the women
who care for him, his virtues are unequalled. When
Roy Richmond carries off his son from the squire's
home to life in a narrow London street, that son is
a petted infant, yet Roy as playfellow more than
compensates for all the luxury left at the grandfather's. 'My father', Harry Richmond tells us,
' could soon make me forget that I was transplanted ;
he could act dog, tame rabbit, fox, pony, and a whole
nursery collection alive . . . When he was at home
I rode him all round the room and upstairs to bed.
I lashed him with a whip till he frightened me, so real
was his barking. If I said '' Menagerie '', he became
a caravan of wild beasts ; I undid a button of his
waistcoat, and it was a lion that made a spring,
roaring at me ; I pulled his coat-tails, and off I went
tugging at an old bear that swung a hind leg as he
turned, in the queerest way, and then sat up, and
beating his breast sent out a mew-moan. Our room
was richer to me than all the Grange while these
performances were going forward. His monkey was
almost as wonderful as his bear, only he was too big
for it, and was obliged to aim at reality in his representation of this animal by means of a number of
breakages ; a defect that brought our landlady on the
scene.' The Sundays of the father and son were
devoted to quieter but not less enthralling entertain-
ments. ' '' Great Will '' my father called Shakespeare,
and '' Slender Billy '', Pitt. The scene where Great
Will killed the deer, dragging Falstaff all over the

park after it by the light of Bardolph's nose, upon
which they put an extinguisher if they heard any of
the keepers, and so left everybody groping about and
catching the wrong person, was the most wonderful
mixture of fun and tears. Great Will was extremely
youthful, but everyone in the park called him
" Father William " ; and when he wanted to know
which way the deer had gone, King Lear (or else my
memory deceives me) punned, and Lady Macbeth
waved a handkerchief for it to be steeped in the blood
of the deer; Shylock ordered one pound of the carcase;
Hamlet (the fact was impressed upon me) offered him
a three-legged stool; and a number of kings and
knights and ladies lit their torches from Bardolph ;
and away they flew, distracting the keepers and
leaving Will and his troop to the deer. That poor
thing died from a different weapon at each recital,
though always with a flow of blood and a successful
dash of his antlers into Falstaff ; and to hear Falstaff
bellow ! But it was mournful to hear how sorry
Great Will was over the animal he had slain. He
spoke like music. I found it pathetic in spite of my
knowing that the whole scene was lighted up by
Bardolph's nose. When I was just bursting out
crying—for the deer's tongue was lolling out and
quick pantings were at his side, he had little ones at
home—Great Will remembered his engagement to sell
Shylock a pound of the carcase ; determined that no
Jew should eat of it, he bethought him that Falstaff
could well spare a pound, and he said the Jew would
not see the difference : Falstaff only got off by hard
running, and roaring out that he knew his unclean

life would make him taste like pork and thus let the
Jew into the trick.' Roy Richmond's irresponsibility
respecting those who are dependent on him is well-
nigh incredible ; yet he keeps hold of our heart-
strings. In that scene near the close of the story where
Squire Beltham makes good his awful threat to strip
Richmond naked of respect even in his own eyes—
to reveal him to himself as the commonest of swindlers
—we look upon Roy, not with the eyes of the man
who has truth and strict justice on his side, but
through those of the high-bred woman who, at the
height of her father's tirade, avows that Richmond
will possess her lifelong devotion. The whole story,
too, is rounded to its conclusion in the scene in which
Harry returns finally to the Grange with the girl long
ago chosen by his grandfather for his wife. As they
approach, the sky hangs red, and, when the house
comes into view, it is wrapped in flames ; fire at the
wings, fire at the centre, no vestige of the home of
generations of Belthams is to be salved. Harry's
father, broken and failing, but consistent to the end,
has been making preparations for Harry and his bride
—' lamps, lights in all the rooms, torches in the hall,
illuminations along the windows, stores of fireworks,
such a display as only he would have dreamed of '.
Once again the price of Roy Richmond's fooling is
to pay. But the comedian himself does not appear
on the stage. Seeking to rescue Dorothy Beltham he
has laid down his life. In final largesse, he has filled,
he has even outdistanced, the rôle of his own
Richmond Roy !

In connexion with Meredith's interest in inter-

national affairs, special attention should be paid
to the exposition in *Harry Richmond* of the German
point of view and the German vision of the English.
England, as revealed to Harry through the eyes of
Ottilia, was growing mindless and arrogant, and
likely only to regain her spiritual standing in Europe
if temporarily overthrown, that in a period of poverty
she might shed her materialism.   Ottilia's professor-
tutor regarded English national development as
being throttled by a married clergy and a mercantile
aristocracy.

CHAPTER VIII

EVENTS OF THE EARLY SEVENTIES
BEAUCHAMP'S CAREER, 1870–1874

WITHIN three months of their marriage George Meredith and his wife had been obliged to write to Dr. Jessopp of their perplexities in regard to Arthur.[1] At the beginning of 1867 the boy of thirteen was transferred from the Norwich Grammar School to an international school at Berne—a school conducted on Pestalozzian lines and having considerable likeness to Weyburn's school in *Lord Ormont and his Aminta*. Here, however, Arthur settled no better than he had done in England.[2] On the following 8 February (1868) a letter of George Meredith's most lovingly accounts for a delay in writing which has been enforced by the two months lost to him over Captain Maxse's election campaign, and suggests that Arthur, if he feels himself too old for the school where he now is, possibly might be moved on to Dresden. 'How much,' says the letter, ' I long to meet you. . . . May God forever bless you, I pray it nightly.'[3]

In 1870 Arthur Meredith is living in the family of a Professor Zeller in Stuttgart, and his father is sending him money, and following him with every kind of affectionate solicitude in regard to a summer vacation visit it has been arranged for the boy to

---

[1] *Letters of George Meredith*, vol. i, p. 167.
[2] Ibid., p. 323.   [3] Ibid., pp. 193–5.

make to Madame Poussielque in Savoy.[1] On the
25th October of that same year a long letter of George
Meredith's to this son, now back in Stuttgart, contains,
with the tenderest care for details of his health and
his clothing, gentle suggestion that youth is better
employed in observing than in pronouncing judgements.[2] Arthur's position is difficult. He is among
Germans, and the Franco-Prussian War has broken
out ; but the father's wisdom is evidently more than
a little aware that the youth's intransigence is general
and not particular. ' The Professor says you do not
consort with Germans at all. I am grieved at this. . . .
If you do not cultivate the people you are living
amongst in your youth, you will fail in having
pleasant places to look back on—landmarks of your
young days ' ; ' You never speak of the other fellows
living with the Professor. Can you make nothing of
them ? ' But, behind the exhortation, gentle as
that is, schemes are being suggested by friends
intimate enough to follow the father's anxiety to
provide this intractable son again with a new chance
and a new environment. Jessopp has proposed, and
John Morley has agreed, that, if Arthur has mastered
enough German, he might enter for the Taylorian
Scholarship in Modern Languages at Oxford.[3] This
is at Christmas 1870 ; and on the 12th June following
George Meredith is sending, with a present for Arthur's
birthday, money for a tour on the Danube or elsewhere, promising, if only finances permit, to be himself

---

[1] *Letters of George Meredith,* vol. i, pp. 207–8 : the eldest
Miss Vulliamy had married Commandant Poussielque of Pont
de Beau Voisin, Savoy.

[2] Ibid., pp. 212–15.   [3] Ibid., pp. 217–18.

in Stuttgart that August. Arthur, at this time, is very anxious to visit Vienna. He is, George Meredith writes, fully aware of his father's objections to his going there ; yet, if he will give his word to behave honourably, that father will no longer oppose the project.[1] This letter, like all the letters to Arthur, breathes unremitting affection ; but it breathes anxiety also. The hope to get to Stuttgart that August is repeated. The only consideration that may prevent is want of funds. His daughter—Marie Eveleen Meredith—had been born two days earlier (10 June 1871) and expenses are many.

In March 1872 Frederick Maxse proposes that Arthur shall be brought to England to sit at a Foreign Office examination for a post of interpreter in China. Payment for the post, if obtained, is small ; but Maxse, like all George Meredith's intimates at this date, is conscious how heavily the novelist is overworking, and is anxious, now there are two babes to support, that the son who is a young man shall begin, at least, to be self-supporting. But the father will not be spared thus at the expense of the son's banishment. George Meredith's negative, on the 21st March 1872, to this proposal is decisive.[2] Nevertheless that letter of refusal to Captain Maxse contains the admission that its writer is wishful particularly not to be thought hard to please in this matter, because he is in fact exceedingly worried about Arthur, and anxious as to openings for his future. George Meredith's letter of the 25th April of that

[1] Ibid., pp. 226–7.
[2] Ibid., p. 235.

year (1872) to Arthur is inherently, as well as incidentally, of special interest. Arthur has written of discarding certain theological beliefs, but has added that the moral value of religion to mankind he is able to perceive. The last clause his father dwells upon rejoicingly, and continues :

' If you have not the belief, set yourself to love virtue by understanding that it is your best guide both as to what is due to others and what is for your positive personal good. If your mind honestly rejects it, you must call on your mind to supply its place from your own resources. Otherwise you will have only half done your work, and that is always mischievous. . . . Look for the truth in everything, and follow it, and you will then be living justly before God. Let nothing flout your sense of a Supreme Being, and be certain that your understanding wavers whenever you chance to doubt that he leads to good. We grow to good as surely as the plant grows to light. And do not lose the habit of praying to the unseen Divinity. Prayer for worldly goods is worse than fruitless, but prayer for strength of soul is that passion of the soul which catches the gift it seeks.

                    Your loving father,
                        George Meredith.' [1]

The incident giving that letter special interest is that it is the last of the letters we possess to Arthur's boyhood. Shortly after this date an eight years' estrangement between the father and son was to ensue. But even so short a summary of their correspondence as I have been able here to give should make very clear to the reader the father's gentleness and consideration. At this point, to trace Arthur

---

[1] *Letters of George Meredith*, vol. i, pp. 236–8.

Meredith's life to its close would be to leap too far
forward in time. It is sufficient to say now that, when
relations were reopened, George Meredith's fatherly
love grew unfailingly with the tax put upon it.

At times during his life George Meredith gave way
momentarily to outbursts of temper. If proof were
needed that these tempers were nerve-storms resulting
from his constant dyspepsia, and from no sourness
of mentality, that proof would be given by the
mellowness of his correspondence in general, and
by the continence of one letter in particular—a
reply to a letter from a friend which had wounded
him most deeply—which is given at length here
because it is not less than a model, in dignity and
gentleness, of how such a letter, if it is to be written
at all, should be written :

'Box Hill, March 23, 1871. My dear ——, I will
answer as plainly as you have written. I cannot but be
shocked and grieved to think of the effect my manner of
speaking has had in clashing with your " opinions, ideas,
and likings ". But that this should prompt you to tell
me that it makes my society seem baneful to you ; and
that only with me do you suffer the consciousness that
you fail to get new strength, and that your complaint of
me is not captious because I am the only friend who has
ever caused you to complain—these are accusations
which point in one direction, that is, to the end of our
intimacy. You consent to say that upon the larger matters
we are one. I have thought so, and have considered the
minor differences too small to dwell on, the possible
expression of them by one or the other of us too mean a
subject for the preciousness of friendship in our short
life to brood on. For I am sensitive, and I likewise have

thought myself here and there roughly used by you.
But I pardoned the offending minute when the hour had
struck, and never thought of identifying the offence with
my friend. I chose to blame myself, as the safer way of
closing a slight wound. It seems that I have been
roughening you for six months. When I last came over to
you I was bright with the happiness of being with you, and
I remember I denounced (as I supposed I might do to a
friend) a poem that struck me as worthless. I spoke like
a man coming off a country-road fasting. It may be too
often my manner. I might well think my friend would
not let it live with him, and that he knew my mind better
than to allow a sense of variance to spring from such
differences in open talk. Possibly a nature that I am
proud to know never ceases in its growth, is passing now
through some delicate stage which finds me importunate ;
or you feel that you have outstripped me, and are
tempted to rank me with the vulgar. I can bring a
thousand excuses for a letter that I have read often to
assure myself it is among the things which are, but
arrive only at the conclusion I have named. We will
see one another as little as we can for two or three years,
and by and by may come together again naturally. And
if not, you will know I am glad of the old time, am always
proud of you, always heart in heart with you on all the
great issues of our life, and in all that concerns your
health and fortunes. I suffer too much to-day to desire
that any explanation should restore us to our past
footing. Almost I am tempted to hope that I am quite
valueless to you, for as I am not a man to send such a letter
as you have just written to me, without deeply weighing
every word in it and probable signification of its burden
to the reader, or without weighing my feelings well
against my friend's, so I am not the man to receive one

without determining to abandon a position that has exposed me to be wounded. What you have permitted yourself to write, and I to quote from you, cuts friendship to the ground. That I should be the only one of your friends ever to have done you harm, is not a nice distinction to reflect on. But I think I have said enough. I have answered you plainly and fully, and as to a sane man master of the meaning of his words and meaning exactly what they commonly convey—I am ever yours faithfully and warmly,

GEORGE MEREDITH.'

Through the years we have now under consideration, on from the end of 1867 in fact, Meredith had been writing *Beauchamp's Career*. By the spring of 1874 it was in John Morley's hands for publication in the *Fortnightly Review*. With regard to the shortening, by one-third of its length, for use as a serial, of what was in the custom of that time a three-volume novel, we have several very interesting letters; and one of these, to Moncure Conway, discusses the chances of the book being issued in America, and explicitly says that *Beauchamp's Career* gives a picture of political life and thought as Meredith had experienced it at the end of the eighteen-sixties in England. There is, of course, no sort of question that the foundation of *Beauchamp's Career* was the election campaign in which Frederick (afterwards Admiral) Maxse stood as Radical candidate for Southampton in 1867—indeed, the first draft of the tale had been written in Maxse's house, Hamble Water, directly that election was over. Beauchamp was known to be taken from Meredith's

I

lifelong friend Maxse himself.[1] But, over and above that, I have in my possession a letter written to me, from Admiral Maxse's son, giving the names of the originals of most of the masculine characters. Blackburn Tuckham, for instance, was William (afterwards Sir William) Hardman, who is so largely addressed in the *Letters of George Meredith*.

If upon no other account, *Beauchamp's Career* would have great value for us to-day in its re-creation of the political atmosphere of three generations ago. When the tale opens, with Beauchamp a boy of fifteen, France is still the hereditary enemy of England, and terror of French invasion is general. This is augmented by distrust of Louis Napoleon and righteous indignation at his cowing of Paris by massacre of unarmed citizens. These feelings have been stirred by Lord Palmerston and *The Times* newspaper into a panic. England is told that it may wake any morning to find that fifty thousand Frenchmen have landed on its shores in the night. The panic grows to ludicrous proportions ; the Militia Bill is passed ; and the death and pageant funeral of the Duke of Wellington aid in turning Englishmen's minds to wars and warlike exploits.[2] Meanwhile Russia has been helping Austria to crush Kossuth and Hungary, and by doing so has induced an anti-Russian alliance between the humanitarian

[1] In 1862 *Modern Love and Poems of the English Roadside* was ' affectionately dedicated to Captain Maxse, R.N.' Thirty years later *Modern Love, a Reprint ; To which is added The Sage Enamoured and the Honest Lady* is inscribed ' To Admiral Maxse, in constant friendship '.

[2] See John Morley's *Life of Richard Cobden*, vol. ii, chap. 5.

and jingo sentiments in England. The powder is stored; Russia crosses the Pruth, and the match is lit. *Beauchamp's Career* pays tribute to ' the daunt-less Lancastrian who thundered like a tempest over a gambling tent, disregarded ',[1] and to the three Quakers who, on the eve of the war, made pilgrimage to the Tzar beseeching him to give way ' for piety's sake '.[2] The tribute of Beauchamp, to John Bright at any rate, is the more valuable in that Beauchamp, like Meredith himself, set out with distinct antagonism to the political school of Cobden and Bright. And the reason for that initial antagonism is not difficult to discover. Both Meredith and Beauchamp refer at times to the middle and mercantile classes as the backbone of England. They force themselves to that concession, and feel their duty done. But their affections were solely for the classes above and below the commercial class. Those above met their taste, those below provided the field for their idealism. The intermediate region represented little more, to their minds, than a dead weight of obstruction. Material wealth, causing increase in materialism, they saw as the curse of England, and permeation with ideas as her crying need. Among those at the top of the social ladder, those satiated with the goods of this world, there were indeed many of dull minds,

---

[1] John Bright.

[2] The account of the three Quakers—Robert Charlton, Henry Pease, and Joseph Sturge—is that they were waiting in St. Petersburg, at the Tzar's request after most hopeful interviews with him, when certain issues of *The Times* arrived which by their inflammatory articles put an end, as they were intended to do, to any possibility of peace.

but these persons recognized mental brilliancy at
least as a social asset. And those at the bottom of
the scale, those who were hungering, were open
enough to ideas. ' Tall talk,' says Everard Romfrey
in *Beauchamp's Career*, ' is their jewelry : they must
have their dandification in bunkum ' ; they listen
agape to all who profess to prescribe for their ills.
Stronghold of intellectual sluggishness, then, was the
prosperous but untraditioned middle class. In short,
the rise of the manufacturing politician appeared
to betoken the rapidly increasing influence of mere
wealth divorced from tradition. And the fact that
the ' cotton-spinner's ' voice first made itself heard
in the interests of peace was likely to obscure for
Meredith and Beauchamp the points of similarity in
their creeds. England's bungling into the Crimean
War occurred, in Beauchamp's view, largely because
' we really had been talking gigantic nonsense of
peace, and of the everlastingness of the exchange of
fruits for money, with angels waving raw-groceries
of Eden in joy of the commercial picture ' ; and the
' George Foxite ' speech of Manchester was easy to
mistake for the trade-at-any-price cry, ' the cry of
the Belly ', wishful to dominate the intellect and
muscle of England.

Beauchamp's Career is George Meredith's single
political novel. The scope of his characters necessi-
tates political allusions in most of his books. But
details of Harry Richmond's parliamentary candidature, or even of Sigismund Alvan's and Diana
Warwick's party opinions, do not constitute a political
novel. National interests in these cases are attributes

of the characters, they are not the pivot on which the characters move. Beauchamp's personal and private concerns, on the other hand, are little but platforms to mount us to the conception of an Englishman passionately moved by political ideas. This tale, Meredith writes, is of one ' born with so extreme and passionate a love for his country that he thought all things else of mean importance in comparison. This day, this hour, this life, and even politics, the centre and throbbing heart of it, must be treated of : men and the ideas of men, which are actually the motives of men in greater degree than their appetites : these are my theme.' This statement of the true theme of the book should be kept in mind by the reader of it, for it provides the corrective to any instinctive disappointment which may be experienced respecting Beauchamp's relations with Cecilia and Jenny. With Renée in Venice he is wholehearted indeed ; but his career then has not opened ; we have only, as it were, material with which his idealism will have to work. And even there we may, if we will, find a foretaste of what is to come in that great scene on the Adriatic, when Beauchamp has had the yacht put about and is refusing to let Renée's brother turn it again towards Venice and Renée's betrothed. For, even in that exalted moment, Beauchamp's mind is accessible to fact. The lover's dream of a world plastic to his wishes has been his for an hour, but Rosamund Culling's reminder that he is financially dependent on his uncle—Everard Romfrey—' strikes his hot brain with a bar as of iron '. And later, with Renée when she has fled from her husband, Beauchamp sets his conviction as to the wider world's dues and claims to confront and subdue his agonized longing. Beauchampism, Meredith tells us, may be said to stand for nearly everything that is the reverse of Byronism.

It hardly needs to be remarked that no one is better qualified than George Meredith to expose in a ludicrous light a youth who should be too consciously attempting the reformation of his elders. In Beauchamp's case Meredith sees no cause for laughter, and the reason he feels none he gives at the outset of the story. Proud of his high spirit and good looks, his uncle Everard would have spoiled Nevil Beauchamp in his childhood, had not the boy's veneration for heroes, both living and dead, held him from conceit. Nevil is a hero-worshipper, obsessed by reverence for men of deeds and incapable therefore of esteeming himself—who has done nothing —highly. Destined by his uncle for the navy, to which he is to be dispatched at the age of fourteen, he expresses a desire to stay longer at school. ' The fellow would like to be a parson ! ' Everard Romfrey ejaculates in high disgust. ' I'd rather enlist for a soldier,' replies Nevil in repudiation of the charge, but despairing of explaining his true motive. Yet to the lady who keeps his uncle's house, his dear friend Rosamund Culling, he confides that, in one particular, parsons are to be envied—they have the time to read history and decide whether Cromwell or Charles I was in the right ! Nevil Beauchamp hates bloodshed, and, to his uncle Everard's mind, comes dangerously near to ' the cotton-spinner's

babble' in speaking of it. He even seems to have
got hold of some Manchester School sarcasms about
the word Glory. 'He said, "I don't care to win
glory; I know all about that; I've seen an old hat
in the Louvre." And he would have Rosamund to
suppose that he had looked on the campaigning
head-cover of Napoleon simply as a shocking, bad,
bald, brown-rubbed old tricorne, rather than as the
nod of extinction to thousands, the great orb of
darkness, the still-trembling gloomy quiver—the
brain of the lightning of battles.' The boy's shrinking
from the prospect of his life in the navy almost
amounted to terror; all the same he returned from
his first voyage, as his uncle had predicted he would,
a gallant sailor. And a year or two later, during the
Crimean War, Edward Romfrey finds himself obliged,
by reports of Nevil's outrunning his duty, to write
to him that what England is in need of is soldiers and
sailors, not suicides. As Beauchamp's great-aunt
sagely points out at this time, trouble would have
been spared if the lad had been allowed to remain
at school and had gone on to college. In an atmosphere
of words, he would probably have been bled of his
plethora of ideas. As it was, they accumulated to
unwieldy proportions. But it is Meredith's favourite
distinction between great-natured and small-natured
persons that the former reverence and the latter
despise what is beyond their understanding; and it
was Beauchamp's safeguard that he was always
finding, in books and in his fellows, more than he
found in himself. His boyhood's choice of Carlyle
for his favourite author was largely based on Carlyle's

obscurity; he ' liked a bone in his mouth to gnaw at ', he said.   Meredith, probably because he had his model Maxse closely before him, has avoided the danger of simplifying Beauchamp to his typical masculine mould.   Gallant and upright as Wentworth and Whitford and Weyburn, Beauchamp has much more complexity.   In *The Tragic Comedians* Meredith has written : ' Men who have the woman in them without being womanised, they are the pick of men,' and we suspect that this generalization had root in his knowledge of Beauchamp.   Lover of all that was gracious and graceful, we are told ' Beauty plucked the heart from his breast ', yet, taking up arms for his less fortunate fellows, he set out on the long task of bringing beauty to the many instead of the few. ' He said " by-and-by " to pleasure, battle to-day.' Rare indeed at the time Meredith was writing *Beauchamp's Career*, Beauchamp's type of character— happily less rare in our own time—is portrayed with perfect success ; one in which disregard of means to ends, and some consequent want of effectiveness, are due, not to conceit, but to over-enthusiastic belief in the immediate capacity for amendment of human institutions.

Rosamund Culling, though a subsidiary character, is a delightful one.   Widow of a distinguished military officer, she is both a gentlewoman and a woman of the world.   Therefore the fact that Beauchamp, who has known and loved her as mistress of his uncle's house from his earliest childhood, should regard his uncle's later marriage with her as a *mésalliance* is strange to eyes of to-day.   Mr. George Trevelyan has remarked

that, when Meredith's thought was out of touch with
the thought of his—Mr. Trevelyan's—generation, it
was usually because Meredith's was ahead. In fundamental matters this is fact. But (my generation
is the same as Mr. Trevelyan's) in matters of convention and custom, between 1870 and 1907, when Mr.
Trevelyan wrote, considerable changes for the better
had taken place. Minor social distinctions were much
less observed. Another small change lay in a different
estimate of age. Lady Charlotte Chillingworth's
desire for marriage with Wilfrid Pole is quickened by
the thought that she has passed the ' fatal ' thirtieth
birthday; when Diana Warwick, disciplined and
initiated, is allowed at last to fall back on the maturely
staid business-man of the book, a man whom we
should have imagined to be fifty years at least, the
reader is astonished to be told he is thirty-three;
in *Beauchamp's Career*, Renée de Croisnel is marrying
the Marquis de Rouaillout when just seventeen.

Beauchamp, who has saved her brother's life in
the Crimea, meets Renée in Venice. Beauchamp is
wounded, and his days are passed with Renée and
Roland gliding in and out of the canals in a gondola
which Renée has dressed in imitation of Carpaccio's
decorations. Renée is like a crystal cup brimming
with the ancient glories, and into her Meredith has
poured the love for Venice evident in many of his
writings, but at its fullest expression in *Beauchamp's
Career*. The poignant beauty of that city of dreams
so encompasses Renée and Beauchamp that the
intensity of their relations there seems never quite
recaptured in the scenes at Tourdestelle. They stand

together, to look back at the Doge's palace glowing like a second sunset north-westward of the dropping splendour on the hills, from the boat in which they, under Rosamund Culling's protection, are to spend their last night before the arrival of Renée's elderly marquis. Beauchamp sleeps on deck, and wakes with the dawn to see the peaks at the head of the Venetian Gulf being kindled to flame ; ' His personal rapture craved for Renée with the second long breath he drew ; and now the curtain of her tent-cabin parted, and greeting him with a half-smile, she looked out. The Adriatic was dark, the Alps had heaven to themselves. Crescents and hollows, rosy mounds, white shelves, shining ledges, domes and peaks, all the towering heights were in illumination from Friuli into farthest Tyrol ; beyond earth to the stricken senses of the gazers. Colour was steadfast on the massive front ranks : it wavered in the remoteness, and was quick and dim as though it fell on beating wings ; but there too divine colour seized and shaped forth solid forms, and thence away to others in uttermost distances where the incredible flickering gleam of new heights arose, that soared, or stretched their white uncertain curves in skylike wings traversing infinity. It seemed unlike morning to the lovers, but as if night had broken with a revelation of the kingdom in the heart of night.'

But the achievement of this book in characterization is, next at least to Beauchamp himself, Everard Romfrey. We are to consider, presently, George Meredith's treatment of egoism in his Prelude to *The Egoist*. And as survivor of that ' grand old

Egoism ' which ' aforetime built the House ' no finer
example than Everard Romfrey is anywhere to be
found. He comes of a long race of fighting earls,
a savour of North Sea foam and piracy about their
earliest history, later, chivalrous knights and leaders
in battle. At the time *Beauchamp's Career* opens,
the then Earl of Romfrey from his topmost tower
could see few spots of land not his own in all that
wide circle. And his brother, the Hon. Everard
(Stephen Denely Craven) Romfrey stands in good
prospect of inheriting the lands and title. He—
Everard—in mind is a medieval baron. He stood
for King, Lords, and Commons, ' Commons he added
out of courtesy.' His real interest is the preservation
of his game. Beside this consideration, all other
matters sink to insignificance ; and it is on the
question of his fellows' attitude towards the Game
Laws that all his partialities or antipathies turn.
Childless and a widower, he adopted his sister's son,
Nevil Beauchamp, as a baby. Throughout, his
affection for Beauchamp is real, but Beauchamp and
Shrapnel defend poachers, and are therefore incon-
testably mad. Everard is, in the old sense of the
word, a gentleman ; his instincts in private life are
everything that Willoughby Patterne's are not.
Indeed Romfrey's nature differs so widely from
Willoughby's that we cannot but question whether
Meredith does not intend the Patternes' comparatively
recent acquisition of wealth and estates to account
for Willoughby's mean-mindedness. Everard Romfrey is as chivalrous to his dependants as to his equals ;
slightly more so, from the tradition that service, in

itself, is a claim. Rosamund Culling dares, without
fear of offence to her ears, probe him as to the grounds
of the fight, in her defence, between the boy Nevil
and a cousin of his, ' sure that he would at all costs
protect a woman's delicacy, and a dependant's, man
or woman.' When Beauchamp is Radical candidate
for Bevisham his uncle almost succeeds in tricking
him into driving into Bevisham beside the rival
candidate. Yet the idea of disinheriting the lad, for
his detested opinions, is hardly entertained by
Romfrey. When Rosamund Culling has become
his wife, and Countess of Romfrey, she compels him,
for her sake and in thought of their unborn child,
to go to apologize to the man he has horsewhipped.
The task is hateful to Romfrey, but when he has
consented to it, he goes without throwing up to
Rosamund at all her share of responsibility for his
original assault. He arrives at Dr. Shrapnel's house
deeply prejudiced against the doctor and all his
belongings ; nevertheless, introduced to the doctor's
niece, Jenny Denham, Romfrey treats her as though
she were Cecilia Halkett, and even recognizes in her
a distinction that Cecilia does not possess. Struggle
between the ideas of Romfrey and Beauchamp
continues through the book ; it is indeed the subject
of the tale. Yet throughout Romfrey appreciates the
quality of his antagonist, and, most of all, when
Beauchamp is conqueror. At the close of the story,
when Beauchamp, who has been at death's door for
weeks, is coming back to life, news of his engagement
to Jenny Denham reaches the earl. ' " Oh, what an
end to so brilliant a beginning," groans Rosamund's

devotion to Beauchamp. "It strikes me, my dear, it's the proper common-sense beginning that may have a fairish end. He hasn't marched on London with a couple of hundred thousand men: no, he hasn't done that," the earl said, glancing back in mind through Beauchamp's career, "and he escapes what Stukely calls his nation's scourge in the shape of a statue turned out by an English chisel. No: we haven't had much public excitement out of him. But one thing he did do: *he got me down on my knees* "."

Dr. Shrapnel, Beauchamp's political mentor and mouthpiece of his ideals, talks Carlylese. The range of his opinions, and of his expression of opinions, is immense. He is in touch with the soul and the springs of the Universe; but he is not wise. A fellow character in *Beauchamp's Career* says of Shrapnel, 'The study of politics should be guided by some light of statesmanship, otherwise it comes to this wild preaching. *These men are theory-tailors, not politicians.*' Is not that phrase the most incisive criticism that has been penned of the Manchester School? It recalls to us also Meredith's deeply sagacious summary of Carlyle, in a letter to Maxse of January 1870. 'I hold that Carlyle is the nearest to being an inspired writer of any man in our times; he does proclaim inviolable law; he speaks from the deep springs of life. All this. But when he descends to our common pavement, when he would apply his eminent spiritual wisdom to the course of legislation, he is no more sagacious nor useful nor temperate than a flash of lightning in a grocer's shop. "I purify the atmosphere," says this agent. " You knock me down, spoil my goods and frighten my family," says the grocer. Philosophy, while rendering his dues to a man like Carlyle and acknowledging itself inferior in activity, despises his hideous blustering impatience in the presence of progressive facts.'

CHAPTER IX

THE IDEA OF COMEDY, 1877
THE EGOIST, 1879
SHORT STORIES, 1877–1879

ON the 8th February 1877 Meredith delivered, at the London Institution, a lecture *On the Idea of Comedy and the Uses of the Comic Spirit*. The time occupied in its delivery was one hour and twenty-five minutes, throughout which time, Meredith's close friend Cotter Morison reports, the audience was deeply attentive, ' no one left the hall.' That report says much for the attractive personality of the lecturer and the beautiful distinctness of his articulation.[1] For the dish that was put before the Institution that day was of a subtlety so refined that most of its delicacy must, inevitably, have gone unrecognized at first tasting. We, since 1897, have had the advantage of being able to read that lecture in the form in which Meredith finally presented it ; yet it is only after several readings and re-readings that the normal intelligence can comprehend the completeness, the precision, the finality, of what is being said. Yet from the first reading the mind is stimulated and entertained ; for there is no difficulty in the language of the essay beyond the difficulty inherent in the subject. Not only is the nature of the Comic itself defined, but the various emotions which may enter into it and transform it are distinguished and inter-related with consummate skill. A more exhaustive

[1] *Letters of George Meredith*, vol. i, p. 271.

treatment is unimaginable. Satire, Irony, Humour
are perfectly delineated, with a hint for each as to its
fitting place in literature and in life. ' The Satirist
is the moral agent, often a social scavenger, working
on a storage of bile. The Ironëist is one thing or
another according to his caprice ; Irony is the humour
of Satire ; it may be savage as in Swift, with a moral
object, or sedate, as in Gibbon, with a malicious . . .
The stroke of the great Humourist is world-wide, with
lights of Tragedy in his laughter.' The survey is
completed by a criticism of the literature of Comedy,
which, in depth and delicacy of comprehension, in
buoyancy and brilliancy of writing, maintains the
extraordinarily high level of the more abstract
portions of the essay. And, most difficult of all in
so genuinely philosophic a disquisition, the Comic
Spirit is in presence throughout ; the atmosphere is
an intellectual banquet, a feast of the sly smile,
where all the notables who have contributed to the
well-spring of human laughter find themselves
assembled, to be distinguished and appreciated as
never before.

The main purpose of the ' Essay on Comedy ' is
to define the quality which Meredith believed to be
the tutelary genius of modern civilization, the touch-
stone of worth to which he brought all his characters
to be tried. To him, the meaning and justification
of individual experience and suffering is each man's
possibility of raising to great stature qualities latent
within him. But no other writer has so fully perceived
and so relentlessly expressed the immensity of that
task. The main theme of his novels is the purification

of rebellious and intemperate youth : a purification
which, to his mind, can only be effected by experience
in the main painful to the natural Ego, by an ordeal
which he invariably conceives as fiery. So fiery that
at times, against the laboriousness of this discipline,
the waste of youth's energy in mastering mere brutish-
ness, even his giant fortitude rebels :

> Not till the fire is dying in the grate,
> Look we for any kinship with the stars.
> Oh, wisdom never comes when it is gold,
> And the great price we pay for it full worth :
> We have it only when we are half earth.
> Little avails that coinage to the old ![1]

But, he says, it is largely because we neglect the
help at hand that our period of stumbling and
unfruitfulness is so prolonged. For closely hovering
over us is a mentor—the Comic Spirit—ready to be
the individual's guardian and guide in the new epoch
on which mankind is entering. Humanity's watchword henceforth is Community ; it is in power of
voluntary co-ordination with his fellows that test of
the individual's effectiveness henceforth will consist.
' If you believe that our civilisation is founded in
common sense (and it is the first condition of sanity
to believe it), you will, when contemplating men,
discern a Spirit overhead ; not more heavenly than
the light flashed upward from glassy surfaces, but
luminous and watchful ; never shooting beyond
them, nor lagging in the rear ; so closely attached to
them that it may be taken for a slavish reflex, until
its features are studied. It has the sage's brows, and

[1] *Modern Love*, iv.

K

the sunny malice of a faun lurks at the corners of
the half-closed lips drawn in an idle wariness of
half tension.   That slim feasting smile, shaped like
the long-bow, was once a big round satyr's laugh,
that flung up the brows like a fortress lifted by gun-
powder.   The laugh will come again, but it will be
of the order of the smile, finely tempered, showing
sunlight of the mind, mental richness rather than
noisy enormity.   Its common aspect is one of un-
solicitous observation, as if surveying a full field and
having leisure to dart on its chosen morsels, without
any fluttering eagerness.   Men's future upon earth
does not attract it ; their honesty and shapeliness
in the present does ; and whenever they wax out of
proportion, overblown, affected, pretentious, bom-
bastical, hypocritical, pedantic, fantastically delicate ;
whenever it sees them self-deceived or hoodwinked,
given to run riot in idolatries, drifting into vanities,
congregating in absurdities, planning shortsightedly,
plotting dementedly ; whenever they are at variance
with their professions, and violate the unwritten but
perceptible laws binding them in consideration one
to another ; whenever they offend sound reason, fair
justice ; are false in humility, or mined with conceit,
individually or in bulk—the Spirit overhead will look
humanely malign and cast an oblique light on them,
followed by volleys of silvery laughter.   That is the
Comic Spirit.'   Meredith's conception is of a spirit,
which is fruit of many minds, revealing to the individual a standard of fitness and proportion for his
conduct, an ideal of bearing, in which aspiration
unrelated to effort is, above all else, exposed as

burlesque. He sees that spirit hovering over each of
us continually, most apparent to the eyes of others
when least visible to our own :

> Oh ! wad some power the giftie gie us
> To see oursel' as ithers see us.

The Comic Spirit is much more than that.   The
vision of Burns's ' ithers ' indeed, though different
in angle, may be as limited as our own.   Yet Meredith
would tell us that to be even beginners in the Comic
Spirit's school, we must be practised in the gymnastic
of mind that can interchange our standpoint with the
standpoint of our neighbours often and effortlessly.
For the Comic Spirit, being intellectual—fruit of
man's mind—can speak to mind only.   If the senses
are uppermost and even temporarily have ' usurped
the station of their issue, mind ', only one way of
teaching is open—the victim must be allowed to run
unchecked upon his course till the rude buffeting
of his fellows wakes him to knowledge of the spectacle
he presents.

Perhaps the most masterly, and certainly the
easiest, presentation of the thought is in the Prelude
to *The Egoist*. That tale is of an English gentleman,
representative of a great house.   That house, like all
others, was raised to its eminence on egoism—
a grand old egoism that by some force of will or of
character outstripped its fellows to found what we
mean by a Family.   But as centuries have passed, and
the characteristics of the rank and file of men have
improved and refined, ever new and more complex
forms of superiority are needed by the representatives
of such a house, if its eminence is to be maintained.

And above all it is necessary that there shall be no
reverting, under a modern veneer, to the ancient
policy of brute-dominion and grab ; no masquerading
of a Norman baron in the guise of a nineteenth-
century gentleman.   In past times the Comic Spirit
has been reverent of an egoism that was sober,
socially valuable, nationally serviceable ; but now
that that day has gone by, and it lurks only in disguises
and under feigned names, she hunts it mercilessly.
Sentimentalism is the egoist's hotbed, and over the
sentimentalist the Comic Spirit watches continually,
analysing much that is termed ' love ' to expose it
as merely self-projection at a fresh angle, a seeking
of the first person in the second.   Sir Willoughby
Patterne returns to Patterne Hall after a three-years'
absence from England.   His constant and adoring
friend, Lætitia Dale, is the first of his acquaintances
that he meets.   He springs from his carriage.   ' " Lætitia Dale ! " he said, he panted.   " Your name is
sweet English music !   And are you well ? " The
anxious question permitted him to read deeply in
her eyes.   He found the man he sought there, squeezed
him passionately, and let her go.'

Willoughby Patterne is the extreme type of the
Comic Spirit's prey ; he is *the egoist* even among
Meredith's characters.   And to Meredith egoism is
what Original Sin was to our forefathers, an initial
condition common to all and only to be outgrown
by prayer and fasting.   In the incident of Lieutenant
Patterne's visit, and in Willoughby's letters before
his return from America, we see him already immersed
in his egoism.   Yet it is almost entirely in connexion

with his love affairs that the Comic Spirit's chase
and exposure of him is presented. For Meredith
conceives of what is called falling in love as the
crucial experience of all his characters. Richard,
Evan, Emilia, and Wilfrid Pole ; Dahlia, Harry
Richmond, Beauchamp, Willoughby, Vernon, Alvan
and Clotilde, Diana, Lord Ormont, and Fleetwood, this is the Ordeal of them all. The day of
a man's captured ideal—the hour when that which
hitherto has been winged, seems stationed and handed
into the individual's grasp in the person of his
beloved—appears to Meredith the test of a man's
worth. It is, he perceives, infinitely more difficult
for any individual to examine the exact nature of
his personal desires, when he can claim that the well-
being of another is involved in their achievement.
Meredith sees the devil lying in ambuscade from
the moment of the incorporation of a second person
in our identity. Even the least imaginative of us,
finding himself single-handed against the opinion of
others, is apt to surmise the possibility that he may
be wrong. But sheltering from blame behind the
mock-heroic that one's wife would be involved, and
one's wife must be above and beyond all criticism,
is a much subtler allurement. There may appear
to be something almost too restrained in the consideration for others, beyond the two selves, of the
Whitworths and Weyburns and Wentworths—' the
practised in self-mastery '—who are Meredith's
heroes ; but in Willoughby's claim, ' We two have
an inner temple where the worship we conduct is
actually an excommunication of the world. This

gives us our oneness, our isolation, our happiness. This is to love with the soul,' one is forced to recognize an attitude which, though it is spiritually suicidal, is far from uncommon.

Certain critics have held that because Willoughby Patterne's exposure convinces us, and is meant to convince us, of the pervadingness of egoism, we are each called on to recognize in Willoughby a counter-part of ourselves. To hold this, is to introduce a standard of realism that is disavowed by Willoughby's author, to miss his conception of Comedy as a distilling apparatus—a condenser. Meredith, for his essay on *The Idea of Comedy*, had been reading and estimating Molière. His aim in *The Egoist* is comic drama in the style of Molière, exposition of a single type-character. Within that limit it has to be judged. And that limit, as Meredith perfectly well knew, is narrow. In May 1879 he wrote of *The Egoist* in a letter, ' As it mainly comes from the head and has nothing to kindle the imagina-tion, I thirsted to be rid of it soon after conception, and it became a struggle in which health suffered ' ; [1] and again, ' It is a comedy with only half of me in it.' [2] These sentences, from George Meredith's own letters, may, we hope, be allowed to dismiss, once and for all, the theory of many critics that *The Egoist* is the greatest of Meredith's novels. Its limits afford practically no scope for the poetic intensity of which the author of *Richard Feverel*, *Sandra Belloni*, and *The Tale of Chloe* was capable

[1] *Letters of George Meredith*, vol. i, p. 297.
[2] Ibid., vol. i, p. 300.

—a fact of which Meredith himself is most fully aware :

> For this the Comic Muse exacts of creatures
> Appealing to the fount of tears ; that they
> Strive never to outleap our human features,
> And do Right Reason's ordinance obey,
> In peril of the hum to laughter nighest.
> But prove they under stress of action's fire
> Nobleness, to that test of Reason highest
> She bows ; she waves them for the loftier lyre.[1]

Nevertheless subsidiary characters of the book possess vitality enough to have served the everyday novelist for half a dozen novels at least. Clara, Vernon, Dr. Middleton, Crossjay, De Craye, even Lætitia herself, have a vivid existence. They are compelled in certain directions by being members of the Egoist's household ; but they have also a full existence of their own, over and above that which is required for the exposure of Willoughby's errors. With the arrival of Dr. Middleton and his daughter at Patterne Hall, and the opening of the battle between Clara's pledged word to Sir Willoughby and her growing distaste for thought of its fulfilment, real characterization may be said to begin. The imminence of Clara's struggle has been conveyed to the reader previously through the eyes of Clara's companions. Young Crossjay, after his first glimpse of her, had run to Lætitia with news of a lady with a merry face and a fondness for the navy ; Vernon Whitford detected her unusual quickness in the uptake ; Willoughby protested overmuch respecting

---

[1] *The Two Masks* (of Melpomene and Thaleia).

her ingenuousness. On one side, irritation too incredulous of the possibility of revolt to acknowledge
itself as uneasiness, on the other blind hopefulness
that the man she had felt attracted by at first must
reassert himself in her lover, such is the situation
between Willoughby and Clara when the drama
begins.

But already, in its earliest beginnings, it has had
an observant spectator. Since Clara's engagement,
Willoughby's cousin and dependant, Vernon Whitford, has been visiting Clara's father. He has
obviously avoided being left alone with her, but from
time to time at meals he has subjected her to a
penetrating gaze. At first meeting, Clara had liked
his eyes, but lately their look had been reminding
her too much of the brooding and apprehension of
a parent bird on the nest. After one at least of her
conversations with Willoughby recently, she has been
conscious of actual relief in Vernon's absence; has
been feeling herself afraid to encounter that look.
When she presently comes to Patterne Hall it is
inevitable that Vernon should sometimes be in her
company. He is a mere adjunct of that household,
liable at any moment to be called on to act as Clara's
retainer in Willoughby's absence. And with him
she soon learns to have no self-consciousness; he is
devoid of Willoughby's graces—is a bad dancer and
an indifferent horseman. As writer of Willoughby's
letters to the press Vernon is most useful, and his
eminence as a scholar and controversialist adds
a distinction to Patterne, parallel in kind to its
reputation for Parisian cooking. He goes on his

way without the smallest pretension, and Clara notices, half-regretfully, that he seldom dissents, in speech, from Sir Willoughby. If it had been possible for Clara to see him with eyes familiar with Meredith's other heroes, she might, from the outset, have been more fully aware of Vernon Whitford's significance. For she learns, in their first interview, that he has been nine and a half hours on foot, walking off irritation with his pupil Crossjay; and at their second encounter she comes on him asleep beneath the double-blossom wild-cherry which Willoughby has already scoffingly named to her as 'Vernon's holy tree'. Now Meredith himself, throughout his life, was the most enthusiastic of walkers, and

> She, the wild white cherry, a tree
> Earth-rooted, tangibly wood,
> Yet a presence, throbbing, alive,[1]

gleamed as a banner and a beacon at the deepest hour of his own experience.

Of Dr. Middleton it has been said that he belongs to the families of *Crotchet Castle* and *Gryll Grange*. The dedication of his 1851 volume of poems bears witness to George Meredith's admiration for his father-in-law; and to Peacock's influence on Meredith's work we have the testimony of no less astute a literary critic than James Thomson. Yet, though a relationship certainly exists, it is collateral rather than in the direct line of descent. Dr. Middleton certainly is at one with Folliott in his respect for the classics and his esteem for good cooking. Their, not very consistent, ideas of woman's nature and right educa-

[1] *A Faith on Trial.*

tion, if we allow for certain modifications of custom
due to difference of date, are almost identical. The
sentence in which Folliott answers the question
whether ladies must be excluded from his resus-
citated Athenian theatre with the men citizens
disgraced by their ignorance of Greek, might be for
style and sentiment Dr. Middleton's: 'Every man may
take in a lady, and she who can construe and metricise
a chorus, shall, if she so please, pass in by herself '.
But, though the manners of Patterne have lost in
robustness, compared with those of Crotchet, they
have gained much in other directions ; and on Meredith's theory that women are what their menkind
make them, substitution of Mrs. Mountstuart, and
Lætitia, and Clara, for Mrs. Folliott, Miss Crotchet,
and Miss Clarinda, is no small testimony to masculine
development. Moreover Dr. Middleton is at his best
and most convincing when the issues under consideration are subtlest. The often-quoted episode of ' An
Aged and a Great Wine ' is good farce, but it does
not compete with the Doctor's adroitness regarding
Willoughby's snappishness to De Craye on the way
to Mrs. Mountstuart's party, or his dialogue with
the ladies Eleanor and Isabel, and Lætitia's father.
Sympathizing, as Dr. Middleton probably would, with
Folliott's way of correcting Eavesdrop's unmannerli-
ness, he, nevertheless, relegates such rough and
ready methods to the correction of Crossjay and his
comrades, and excels in subtler means of rebuke
for his equals.

Horace De Craye is the most delightful of Meredith's Irishmen. As soon as his baggage comes in

view, a breeze seems to stir the rarefied atmosphere of Patterne, and this promise of refreshment is not belied. Accident has favoured De Craye beforehand with an introduction to Clara, and she has acknowledged his charm ; for, within the short space of an hour, they have quickened acquaintance to intimacy, and Lætitia Dale has felt scandalized by the change of aspect in one who, so shortly before, had talked of despair. Clara is soon to realize that De Craye is not the sustaining, strong man of her dreams—ideal for anchorage—that he is, in fact, but ' a holiday character '. Yet, outwearied as she is by iterations of deaf misunderstanding, she is ready to estimate highly a gift for responsiveness and accordant chiming : over-highly, perhaps. Yet there is a delicacy and elasticity in De Craye's sympathy with her changes of mood, not easy to over-estimate. His instinctive actions for sparing her pain are almost invariably accurate. He can appreciate her frankness in stating the nature of her influence over Crossjay ; and realize that her accent on the word ' marriage ', within a few weeks of her own, betokens a wider idea than wish for mere exchange of lovers. His gay tactfulness is delightful in contrast with Willoughby's rigidity, and also to some extent in relation to Vernon Whitford's starchiness. For, though there can be no question that in Whitford, and Redworth, and Weyburn, Meredith draws his ideal type, he keeps a warm place in his heart for worldlings, wanting in the steadfastness and rectitude of his heroes, if only they possess a keen sense of fitness. These may not be of the Kingdom exactly,

but they are secured, at any rate, from the Outer
Darkness by the fact that their intelligence is habitu-
ally playing and responding over an area of feelings
and interests outside their own. They may not be
great, but the windows of such souls as they possess
are open to life.

Clara Middleton vacillates, till what is little more
than a fortunate accident puts her on the right path.
She belongs to Cecilia Halkett's family ; but she is
capable of robuster growth—not so much of developing strength of her own as of learning to recognize
her weakness and desire its corrective. She longs
to be rescued from Willoughby, yet she does not
accept the lift out of circumstances his first rival
offers. We are given to understand that her allegiance
to Vernon comes of her recognition that she is at
fault in character, as well as in circumstance. That
is, she has achieved some self-knowledge and humility,
which, for Meredith, are the necessary groundwork
of aspiration ; and her misdemeanours are pardoned.
To no member of the masculine sex would her author
have granted so easy escape ! The reader's attention
would have been called to the fact that flight from
one form of spiritual dependence to another form is
but postponement. But, in relation to women,
Meredith sometimes allows his chivalry to override
the relentlessness of his logic. Women, he says,
are the creations of men ; they are scarcely account-
able for weakness and cowardice induced by their
master's requirements. The marvel is that they
show any courage at all. Vacillating desires for
freedom and righteousness are the most a fair-minded

man critic finds himself able to demand from them.
And these are sufficient ; because they are an earnest
of what one day is to be. Clara, in her resistance of
Willoughby and De Craye, and her appreciation of
Vernon, has shown both some courage and considerable perception. Her creator forbears to read her
his whole homily.

*The House on the Beach, The Case of General Ople
and Lady Camper,* and *The Tale of Chloe* appeared in
the *New Quarterly Magazine* for January 1877, July
1877, and July 1879, respectively. That is, they
belong to the period which produced ' The Essay
on Comedy ' ; and in subtlety of thought and delicacy
of workmanship they are close to that essay's level.
Relatively to the profoundly tragic *Tale of Chloe*,
the two earlier stories are comedy, yet in *The House
on the Beach*, at any rate, the ' loftier muse ' comes
closely in her sister's wake. The intermingling of
laughter and tears in that story is the more remarkable
in view of the coarseness of instrument from which
such gradation of tone is obtained ; for *The House
on the Beach* is a study of lower middle-class persons
in a lower middle-class setting. Tinman, its central
character, is a mean-minded ex-tradesman, but now
socially-aspiring Bailiff, of the Cinque Port of Crikswich. Tinman is almost without a redeeming quality,
and in tones of the mock-heroic, well suited to his
bombastic pretensions. Meredith plays with him as
a cat plays with a mouse. He is revealed as even
more sordid than his surroundings, and his surroundings, of vilias in five feet of garden ' with titles of
royalty and bloody battles ', are trumpery enough.

'There was nothing in Crikswich to distract the naked pursuit of health.' At the time of his friend Van Diemen Smith's return from Australia, Tinman is obsessed with a scheme for taking advantage of his office of Bailiff of Crikswich to present an address to Queen Victoria on the occasion of the marriage of one of her daughters. Towards this end, he attitudinizes daily, for hours, before a looking-glass. And Van Diemen Smith, arriving at Crikswich late one evening, walks into a hired mirror which, because of its insufficient reflecting powers, is being sent back, from Tinman's house, to its owner. Van Diemen is large-minded and warm-hearted. It is difficult to believe that there can ever have been real relationship between him and Tinman. But he has been long years away in Australia ; and in those years his love for England has been winding itself with thoughts of the only acquaintance who remains to him there. Moreover Tinman's existence has enabled him partially to explain to himself his long home-sickness. Van Diemen now has wealth, and he has a daughter. He also has an old secret known to Tinman. Tinman covets the daughter and the wealth ; and uses his knowledge of the secret in order to secure them. Van Diemen's strange clinging to Tinman, in spite of these developments, is partly due to the tendency of a generous nature to credit others with its own quality, but even more to the fact that the 'crime' of his youth is on his nerves—he will not look it in the face. Terror of it and its penalties, is the under-side of the tenacity of early impressions which enables him to retain affection

for Tinman. Moreover he has been living long in
a land where men's energies are absorbed in wrestling
for necessities, and sentiment and imagination have
had to maintain themselves on memory. The
comedy of a situation which puts the giant-like Van
Diemen in the hands of such a pigmy as Tinman is
obvious enough ; but Meredith would have us realize
that there is material for tragedy too. And this lies
in Van Diemen's surrender to irrational, unintel-
lectualized, feeling. Vulnerable at one point only,
his obsession of feeling on that point brings him near
to commission of a genuine crime. Under sway of
his nerves, he comes close to delivering his daughter
in marriage to Tinman. That horror is averted,
and a true lover's path opened, by a furious gale
which engulfs Tinman's house on the beach. Tinman,
as the great storm begins, terrified for his property
and stung by checks in his pursuit of Annette Van
Diemen, writes, and addresses to the military authorities, his long-threatened accusation of Annette's
father. That task is done. But the fiends of ship-
wreck are abroad, and sleep in that house is impossible. To distract himself from the raging storm,
Tinman goes to his wardrobe and takes out the
court suit. He puts it on, and hides himself from the
reality of the tempest in imagination of his splendours.
Thus insulated, he lies down, and can sleep. He
wakes, the next morning, to find the waves crashing
through his house, its walls tumbling, and himself
cut off from the land. This material embodiment
of the spiritual forces which have so long been
battering against Tinman's falseness is eminently

characteristic of George Meredith's thought. His immediate subject-matter may be fantastic, but the angle at which he sets it ensures upon it a strong, steady light. Crikswich may occupy the centre of the stage ; but surrounding it is the ocean.

Of *The Case of General Ople and Lady Camper* it is enough to say that it is, perhaps, the flower of Meredith's humour, and that it gives the main tenets of its author's philosophy in miniature. The exquisite fun of the tale lies in Lady Camper's compulsion of General Ople from faults of omission to those of commission—the swiftness with which she drives him along the lines of his tendencies.

It is, however, in *The Tale of Chloe* that the high-water mark of the short stories is reached. The beginning of the tale is not easy reading, but as a whole it is perfected in a way that is rare in Meredith's work. Chloe's character is one of the profoundest of Meredith's creations, the subtlety and intensity of its conception being the more wonderful for its slightness of outline. The scene of the story is an eighteenth-century spa, presided over by a certain Mr. Beamish, a philosophical beau, who by skilful rules and conventions raises the manners of the society under his care to an unusual pitch of decorum. Beamish undertakes, for the space of a month, charge of the rustic girl-wife of a middle-aged duke, whom her husband desires to see something of the fashionable world, without running the least risk of contamination. Beamish has no fear of not being able to meet the conditions, and he welcomes the Duchess Susan, and provides as her

personal attendant a lady of good birth, who is
known as Chloe. The confidence that Mr. Beamish
reposes in Chloe is unlimited. Years ago she had
sacrificed her estate to a faithless lover, and since
his supposed death she has lived, penniless, at
the Wells. She has ' died for love ', and where
love is concerned she is ' a ghost, an apparition,
a taper '. Yet her spirit is the flame of the Wells ;
she has heart for all its affairs—' the wit and sprightli-
ness of Chloe were so famous as to be considered
medical. She was besieged for her company ; she
composed and sang impromptu verses, she played
harp and harpsichord divinely, and touched the
guitar and danced—danced like the silvery moon
on the waters of the mill-pool.' She is a perpetual
cordial, and, though the outline of her story is known,
no one thinks of pitying her. The strength of her
love in the past is revealed by her uncrippled rising
from the wreck of her hopes. Fountain of good
to her comrades, in the midst of her final ordeal she
appears the most light-hearted and uncalculating.
Superior to the frailties common round her, Chloe
is yet throbbing with every pulse of humanity ;
she is so warmly, simply, human that even her daily
charge, Susan, has only rare glimpses of a quality
that overawes. Romantic and rational, solitary
and social, indomitable in purpose, Chloe has won
to her marvellous insight through feeling so sword-
edged that it has pierced every obstruction. The
rarity of her nature lies in its combination of exquisite and invigorating vitality with aloofness of
spirit. The Duchess Susan is of good heart, but she

L

is rebellious against the rules of the Wells and all for Nature as promising her most enjoyment. She puts her intelligence to sleep, and relies on Chloe for the alarum. She has no desire to exchange her material attractions for intangible ones. Caseldy, Chloe's faithless lover, returns to the Wells, not, as Mr. Beamish and others suppose, to seek Chloe, but in pursuit of the Duchess Susan. Chloe, from the first moment, sees how matters stand; but her love for Caseldy is intense, and she allows herself one month of rejoicing in his mere presence, increasing her care of her charge, never failing in gentleness to Caseldy, and breaking out in scorn of Mr. Camwell, her ardent young champion, when he dares to put what she knows into words and try to inform her of Caseldy's arrangements for eloping with Susan. Chloe's knowledge of every plan and counter-plan, her surrender of life, her conquest of personal pain, endow her with almost unearthly serenity. Her imagination enables her to sympathize both with the woman who supplants her and the man who deceives. 'She made her tragic humility speak thankfully to the wound that slew her. " Had it not been so, I should not have seen him," she said. Her lover would not have come to her but for his pursuit of another woman. She pardoned him for being attracted by that beautiful transplant of the fields : pardoned her likewise. " He when I first saw him was as beautiful to me. For him I might have done as much." ' There is no smallest taint of revenge in Chloe's decision to die ; she vows herself to her course to save a younger woman from ruin. ' Far away

in a lighted hall of the West, her family raised hands
of reproach. They were minute objects, keenly
discerned as diminished figures cut in steel. Feeling
could not be very warm for them, they were so small,
and a sea that had drowned her ran between ; and
looking that way she had scarce any warmth of
feeling save for a white *rhaiadr* leaping out of broken
cloud through blanched rocks, where she had climbed
and dreamed when a child. The dream was then of
the coloured days to come ; now she was more
infant in her mind, and she watched the scattered
water broaden, and tasted the spray, sat there drinking the scene, untroubled by hopes as a lamb, different
only from an infant in knowing she had thrown off
life to travel back to her home and be refreshed.
She heard her people talk ; they were unending
babblers in the water-fall. Truth was with them,
and wisdom. How, then, could she pretend to any
right to live ? ' In this, Chloe's farewell to earth,
the delicate atmosphere of detachment which per-
vades the whole of the story is wrought to perfection.
The artificialities surrounding the drama, the small-
ness of the stage, are used with consummate art to
make it more poignant. That group of tiny figures
waving impotent arms in the West is clear yet far,
actual yet remote, as a scene in some convex old
mirror.

CHAPTER X

THE TRAGIC COMEDIANS, 1880
SOME EVENTS, 1881–1884
DIANA OF THE CROSSWAYS, 1884–1885

THE difficulty, already alluded to, of deciding
the relative merits of Meredith's novels is largely
due to the very wide range of his interests, and the
fact that he seldom mines twice in the same region.
Many, perhaps most, of his stories have foundation
in actual events. In *The Tragic Comedians* he has
selected a subject the main incidents of which are so
well known that he is, as he says, confined ' to the
bare railway line of the story '. The story is that
of Ferdinand Lassalle and Helène von Dönniges ;
nothing, Meredith says, has been added to it—nothing
invented. Nor does the literalness apply to the
incidents merely ; much of the dialogue is taken from
an account of the whole episode written in after life
by the heroine of it.[1] The title of the book, *The
Tragic Comedians*, in itself might serve as the subject
for an essay. Characters of few men, says Meredith,
are of ' a stature and complexity calling for the
junction of the two Muses to name them '. The
character of Ferdinand Lassalle, known in the story
as Sigismund Alvan, is of this stature. Yet in one
respect his acts are ' lividly ludicrous ', and he comes

[1] *Meine Beziehungen zu Ferdinand Lassalle*, by Frau von
Racowitza.

to a lurid end. He is of the *tragic* comedians, those
whose histories reveal some huge discrepancy which
if it be not interrogated, ' to distinguish where
character strikes the note of discord with life,' will
make man appear as the plaything of circumstance.
That man does not thus appear to Meredith, that to
his view fatality always finds first footing in an
avoidable flaw of character, is the point in which
he joins issue with his greatest contemporary
among novelists—Thomas Hardy. *The Tragic
Comedians*—one of Meredith's most brilliant pieces
of writing—opens with a discussion of the word
' fantastical ', and a declaration of its fittingness to
' that wandering ship of the drunken pilot, the
mutinous crew, and the angry captain, called Human
Nature '. Alvan and his lady ' will pass under this
word as under their banner and motto. Their acts
are incredible ; they . . . drove their bark in a manner
to eclipse historical couples upon our planet . . . The
last chapter of them is written in red blood, and the
man pouring out that last chapter was of a mighty
nature, not unheroical, a man of the active, grappling
modern brain, which wrestles with facts to keep the
world alive, and can create them to set it spinning.
A Faust-like legend might spring from him ; he had
a devil. He was the leader of a host, the hope of
a party, venerated by his followers, well hated by his
enemies, respected by the intellectual chiefs of his
time, in the pride of his manhood and his labours
when he fell. And why this man should have come
to his end through love, and the woman who loved
him have laid her hand in the hand of the slayer, is

the problem we have to study, nothing inventing, in
the spirit and flesh of both '.

Clotilde von Rüdiger (Helène von Dönniges) is a
member of the smaller German aristocracy, by which
Sigismund Alvan is abhorred as a demagogue and
a Jew. But the period (1862–1864) is revolutionary in
society as in political life, and Clotilde is renowned as
the most original of her set. Young as she is, her
reputation for brilliancy is great in all the circles she
touches, whether in Germany, Italy, or the French
Riviera. But her flights of daring are almost entirely
confined to intellectual regions, and her family—
consisting of father, a gouty general ; mother, a faded
beauty ; and negligible sisters—willingly ministers to
her self-esteem. Her reading, Meredith tells us, is
' an interfusion of philosophy skimmed, and realistic
romances deep-sounded ', but she belongs to a country
where literature is seriously esteemed and appreciated,
where there is real traffic in ideas. Her talk of
Plutarch and Pompey with her partner at the Berlin
ball is perfectly genuine, though it would be difficult
to imagine an Englishwoman indulging in it. And
this fact, of her intellectual attainments, needs to be
borne carefully in mind ; because, except in the
scenes where he shows her with Alvan, Meredith is
guilty of a prejudice in his treatment of Clotilde, and
over-analysis of motive, which obscures her positive
qualities. It is, of course, part of his purpose to show
her strong in Alvan's presence, weak when she is
alone ; and history is with him here. But there is
the further fact to reckon with, that, long before they
have met, Alvan hears of her as his match, and later,

in spite of clear vision of her failings, continues to feel her worth his winning. Meredith's attitude to Clotilde is the reverse of his normal attitude to women —the magnanimous attitude just spoken of in reference to Clara Middleton and shortly to prove more marked still in regard to Diana of the Crossways. Clotilde has far more forcible opposition than either Clara or Diana has to contend with, yet little or nothing is allowed by her author to her fears ; she is labelled craven at almost her first sign of instability. The reason of this is not far to seek. Meredith is in love with Alvan exactly as he is in love with Diana. He sees in both these characters, or attributes to them, a power of passion that raises them high above their fellow men, and he scorns those who, having been in presence of this power, fail to cling to it as divine. Diana's lover is required to recognize it as covering an offence against the deepest mutual interest of their lives ; Alvan's girlish bride-elect, fortified by her memory of it, must turn from bewilderment at the inconsistency of her lover's actions, and immediately develop power to surmount the brutal opposition of her parents. Is not this, combined with their author's continual insistence on the relative inferiority of Dacier and Clotilde, something very like special pleading ? No one could lay more emphasis than Meredith has elsewhere laid on the fact that it is the task of love, worthy the name, to translate itself into considerate and imaginative action ; moreover, he has written a poem entitled *The Burden of Strength.* In *Diana of the Crossways* Meredith is in love with his heroine and despises Dacier ; here he is in love with

Alvan, and Alvan alone. The characters are of course
historical, and it is not intended to suggest there can
be any doubt which was the greater of nature ; yet
would not Meredith's tribute to Lassalle have been
higher, if he had abstained from pressing his points
so severely against the woman of Lassalle's choice ?
Also, although Helène's conduct is not justified either
by her own or any other version of the story, these
agree in laying more stress than Meredith does on
Lassalle's earlier relations with women, on the
treachery of his friends, and on the degree of Helène's
physical collapse under her father's brutality.[1]

Except, however, for the interests of historical
justice, what Meredith has left undone in *The Tragic
Comedians* is not of much moment ; what he has done
is so great. It is among the best of his novels ; the
theme calls for that poetic treatment in which he is
most himself. The characters and incidents ready to
his hand were vivid ; his task was to provide the
atmosphere in which they moved. And in this he
has succeeded to perfection in his drawing of Alvan ;
' Behind the veil of our human conventions,' says
Alvan to Clotilde, ' power is constant as ever, and to
perceive the fact is to have the divining rod—to walk
clear of shams . . . It is the soul that does things in
this life, the rest is vapour ' ; and Meredith has made
us realize him as one whose grasp on life and reality
compelled submission. Of his place in European
politics little is said. But the facts are part of his

---

[1] There are numerous German authorities on the subject, but
a fair summary of the case is given in English in *Ferdinand
Lassalle and Helène von Dönniges : A Modern Tragedy*, by
Elizabeth E. Evans.

background, only subdued, that the man himself may be seen greater than anything he has done. He appears first in the fourth chapter of the book, a scene which sets the pace for the whole story, and it is the pace that kills. Alvan and Clotilde have been matter of surmise to one another for a year ; at last they are in the same room, in Berlin. Clotilde introduces herself with a contradiction as to the character of Hamlet. Alvan, turns to her, shakes off his masculine companions as other men might shake off a fly. In the midst of a crowd they are alone. ' " Hamlet in due season," said he . . . " I shall convince you." She shook her head. " Yes, yes ; an opinion formed by a woman is inflexible ; I know that : the fact is not half so stubborn. But at present there are two more important factors ; we are not at Elsinore. You are aware that I hoped to meet you ? " " Is there a periodical advertisement of your hopes ?— or do they come by intuition ? " " Kollin was right ! The ways of the serpent will be serpentine. I knew we must meet. It is no true day so long as the goddess of the morning and the sun-god are kept asunder. I speak of myself, by what I have felt since I heard of you." " You are sure of your divinity ? " " Through my belief in yours ! " They bowed, smiling at the courtly exchanges. " And tell me," said he, " as to meeting me ? . . ." She replied : " When we are so like the rest of the world, we may confess our weakness." " Unlike ! for the world and I meet and part : not we two." Clotilde attempted an answer : it would not come. She tried to be revolted by his lording tone, and found it strangely inoffensive. His

lording presence and the smile that was like a waving
feather on it compelled her so fully to submit to
hear, as to put her in danger of seeming to embrace
this man's rapid advances. She said: " I first heard of
you at Capri." " And I was at Capri seven days after
you had left." " You knew my name *then* ? " " Be
not too curious with necromancers. Here is the date,
March 15th. You departed on the 8th." " I think
I did. That is a year from now." " Then we missed :
now we meet. It is a year lost. A year is a great
age ! Reflect on it and what you owe me. How
I wished for a comrade at Capri ! Not a ' young
lady ', and certainly no man. The understanding
Feminine was my desire—a different thing from the
feminine understanding, usually. I wanted my
comrade young and fair, necessarily of your sex, but
with heart and brain ; an insane request, I fancied,
until I heard that you were the person I wanted. In
default of you I paraded the island with Tiberius,
who is my favourite tyrant." ' He describes the
passages between him and Tiberius, who, at his
suggestion, attacks the patricians, while a plebeian
demagogue chronicles the struggle in which he, Alvan,
is destined to fall. Clotilde enters into the extravagance and comments, ' You died bravely ? ' He
replies that bodily death by that sapphire sea and
under that sapphire sky was easier to meet than the
second death of missing, by so few days, a gold-haired
Lucretia. He questions her abruptly : ' " Tell me
frankly—the music in Italy ? " " Amorous and
martial, brainless and monotonous." " Excellent ! "
his eyes flashed delightedly, " O comrade of comrades !

that year lost to me will count heavily as I learn to value those I have gained. Yes, brainless ! There, in music, we beat them, as politically France beats us. No life without brain ! The brainless in Art and in Statecraft are nothing but a little more obstructive than the dead. It is less easy to cut a way through them. But it must be done, or the Philistine will be as the locust in his increase, and devour the green blades of the earth. You have been trained to shudder at the demagogue ?" "I do not shudder," said Clotilde.'

Much of the skill of the scene lies in its interthreading of the near and the far, its mingling of abstract and personal. The 'you and I' of ordinary lovers would have been ludicrously inadequate here ; yet an overweight of intellect would have injured the intensity of effect, which is the keynote of the whole. Alvan, pouring forth his thoughts, checks himself at the close of one of his outbursts with the remark : ' " You leave it to me to talk." "Could I do better ? " "You listen sweetly." "It is because I like to hear." " You have the pearly little ear of a shell on the sand." " With the great sea sounding near it." ' Alvan drew closer to her. ' " I look into your eyes and perceive that one may listen to you and speak to you. Heart to heart, then ! Yes, a sea to lull you, a sea to win you—temperately, let us hope : by storm, if need be. My prize is found ! " ' The giant who, heretofore, has conquered all hearts, his own untouched, trembles in the hands of this girl—his ' golden-crested serpent ', his ' red fox ', his ' shining-haired Lucretia '. Their skimming discussions are like swallow-flights from the

nest beneath the eaves to the surface of the stream.
Their talk is of Heine, with whom Alvan has lived ;
of politics, of Paris, of Italy, of wine, and of Shakespeare ; and last, but not least, of Alvan himself.
He vivifies all that he touches. ' There was a bell in
everything for him ; Nature gave out her cry and
significance was on all sides of the universe . . . Where
Clotilde had really thought, instead of flippantly
tapping at the doors of thought, or crying vagrantly
for an echo, his firm footing in the region thrilled her ;
and where she had felt deeper than fancifully, his
wise tenderness overwhelmed.'

The surrounding guests realize that the love-god is
at work among them—a presence irresistible. Alvan's
love affairs are caught up to the plane of his politics.
His love is volcanic, and the sun and moon and stars
are pressed into its service. The hours race onward
to the morning : Alvan will conduct Clotilde to her
home. ' He laughed to hear her say, in answer to
a question as to her present feelings : " I feel that
I am carried away by a centaur ! " The comparison
had been used to him before.' Their eclipse is afar,
but it is as if a shadow crept to the edge of their sun.
' " No," said he, responding to a host of memories to
shake them off, " no more of the quadruped man !
You tempt him, may I tell you that ? Why now, this
moment, at the snap of my fingers, what is to hinder
our taking the short cut to happiness, centaur and
nymph ? One leap and a gallop, and we should be
into the morning, leaving night to grope for us,
parents and friends to run about for the wits they lose
in running. But no ! no more scandals. That silver

moon invites us by its very spell of bright serenity
to be mad ; just as when you drink of a reverie, the
more prolonged it is, the greater the readiness for
wild delirium at the end of the draught. But no ! "
his voice deepened—" the handsome face of the orb
that lights us would be well enough were it only
a gallop between us two. Dearest, the orb that lights
us two for a lifetime must be taken all round, and
I have been on the wrong side of the moon : I have
seen the other face of it—a visage scored with regrets,
dead dreams, burnt passions, bald illusions, and the
like, the like !—sunless, waterless, without a flower !
It is the old volcano land : it grows one bitter herb :
if ever you see my mouth distorted, you will know I am
revolving a taste of it ; and as I need the antidote
you give, I will not be the centaur to win you, for that
is the land where he stables himself ; yes, there he
ends his course, and that is the herb he finishes by
pasturing on." '

No determination could, we feel, be wiser or more
finely expressed, yet it brings us in sight of the rock
on which these two founder. Alvan, irresistible while
he holds straight on his course, sacrifices his single-
mindedness in the desire to win social advantages over
and above his bride. Accredited good citizenship
becomes his ambition for the first time in his life. He
is deeply in love with Clotilde ; but he desires in-
creasingly to have, with her, a wife and a marriage
unexceptionable in the eyes of the world. In effort
to compass that desire he comes to his death. And
Europe mourns at his tomb. He is killed in a duel,
and much of the fault, Meredith would say most of it,

is Clotilde's. Yet so godlike a figure is he, that to
have been claimed for his mate makes her immortal.
And, after all, we may consent to let ' the woman ',
' poor Clotilde ', serve as his scapegoat ; for has not
Meredith himself, in another context, detected and
exposed identically the same error as Alvan's, where
of Beauchamp with Renée he says : ' He committed
the capital fault of treating her as his equal in passion
and courage, not as metal ready to run into the mould
under temporary stress of fire.'

During the winter of 1879–1880 George Meredith
had been more than usually unwell ; for some time,
indeed, unable to do any work. In the autumn of
1879 his children, William and Marie, both had had
whooping-cough and their father had caught it. By
May of 1880, however, he was considerably better,
able to welcome the Sunday Tramps at Dorking
station and walk with them to Leith Hill,[1] and to
write long, spirited letters to Robert Louis Stevenson.
From October of 1880 to February 1881 *The Tragic
Comedians* was appearing serially in the *Fortnightly
Review*, and in January of 1881 it was published in
book form.   Will Meredith had begun going to

---

[1] ' Leslie Stephen comes down to me three or four times in the
year, with other friends calling themselves " The Sunday
Tramps ", who escape from the dreary London Sabbath once
a fortnight and take a walk of between 20 and 30 miles. When
I was in health I was of the pedestrian party. Now I have to
meet them on the hills half way from home, or less. They dine
with me and start for London at 10 p.m. They are men of
distinction in science or literature ; tramping with them one has
the world under review, as well as scenery. Leslie is acknowledged captain of the band.' Letter from George Meredith,
8 April 1882, *Letters of George Meredith*, vol. ii, p. 338.

Westminster School in 1880, and for the Easter of
1881 he brought home with him to Box Hill his
schoolfellow—Theodore [1]—son of George Meredith's
own long-time friend, James Cotter Morison. But, for
George Meredith, the real event of the year 1881 was
the reopening of communication between himself and
Arthur. On June 18th a visitor made known to him
the news of Arthur's having been ill at Lille and having
had to consult a lung specialist. On June the 19th
a long letter hastened from Box Hill, exquisitely gentle
in its manner of proffering help, from a father who,
though writing himself down as a failure, trusts that
long years of toil at his craft may have fitted him to
be of service now to a son who is taking to literature
as a profession. Arthur is begged to come away from
Lille and rest completely for a year, spending that
year at Box Hill, in the George Merediths' spare bedroom at night and writing with his father in the chalet
at the top of the garden by day. Marie and Will, and
their delight in thought of a big brother who may be
coming home, are described. In short, the letter
makes clear the warm place in family life that is open
and waiting. Money, too, is offered, but with a
delicacy that is almost trepidation ; for evidently
this prospect of intercourse is too precious to the
father's heart to be endangered by even the most
loving precipitancy. On June the 23rd Arthur's
reply is received, and that day his father writes to
him again, this time an even longer, and a more out-
spokenly loving, letter. No repining that Arthur has

[1] Now Sir Theodore Morison, K.C.S.I., K.C.I.E., Principal of
Armstrong College.

not fallen in with the Box Hill scheme is shown ; on the other hand, Arthur's ideas of mountain or sea air are warmly commended, and the relative merits of Malaga and Davos Platz most carefully estimated. Rejoicing that the money which Arthur has lately inherited from a relative of his mother's is more than George Meredith had thought it to be, is warmly expressed. And then, in referring to Tom Taylor's death, come the words ' You may not have seen a sonnet I wrote on him in " The Cornhill Magazine ". Sometimes it used to strike me that writings of mine might fall under your eye '. What a vision of the aching of those years, empty of any word from his son, that sentence calls up ! ' We have ', the letter continues, ' been long estranged, my dear boy, and I awake from it with a shock that wrings me. The elder should be the first to break through such divisions, for he knows best the tenure and the nature of life. But our last parting gave me the idea that you did not care for me ; and, further, I am so driven by work that I do not contend with misapprehension of me, or with disregard, but have the habit of taking it from all alike as the cab-horse takes the whip. Part of me has become torpid. The quality of my work does not degenerate ; I can say no more. Only in my branch of the profession of letters the better the work the worse the pay, and, also, it seems, the lower the esteem in which one is held for it.' [1]

Through much of the autumn of 1881 George Meredith was again ill, and being treated by Hutchinson for some kind of spinal affection. At the end of

---

[1] *Letters of George Meredith*, vol. ii, pp. 352 and 355.

July 1882 he started to take a cure at Evian, travelling afterwards with Arthur Meredith in Italy, and not getting back to England until mid-September. Before starting for this journey Meredith wrote asking John Morley, on the ground of Morley's affection for his children, to be conjointly with Justin Vulliamy executor of his Will. In November, of 1882, Meredith was able to report to Frederick Maxse that the Avalon douches had been of immense benefit to him, and that he is vigorously at work on, he is ashamed to say, a volume of poems. This volume was, of course, *Poems and Lyrics of the Joy of Earth* which was published by Messrs. Macmillan early in 1883. The summer of 1883 was again, as full summer was apt to be, a bad period for Meredith. For years past he had grown, physically, more and more dependent upon bracing weather. That autumn, however, he was at work again very hard on a novel that was promised to appear in the *Fortnightly Review* in the following April or May—a novel which was destined to alter, for ever, his position in the eyes of the English public. That novel was, George Meredith stated to friends more than once, based on a real incident in the life of Mrs. Caroline Norton ; and it was this accident of reference to the story of a novelist and a beauty not long dead,[1] rather than Meredith's work upon it, that gave the book its extraordinary reception. Chapters I–XXVI of *Diana of the Crossways* appeared in the *Fortnightly Review* in 1884, and the complete book, of forty-three chapters, was published in

[1] Mrs. Caroline Elizabeth Sarah Norton, Richard Brinsley Sheridan's granddaughter, had lived till 1877.

M

the following year. And within that year no less than three editions of it had been published and exhausted. That is, in the year 1885, Meredith found himself a popular novelist.

Manifestly Diana Warwick's history is founded upon that of Caroline Norton, one of the three notably beautiful granddaughters of Sheridan who had been immensely admired in mid-nineteenth-century English society, and popular also as poet and novelist. Mrs. Norton's marriage was not happy, and her husband brought a divorce suit against her, citing the then Prime Minister, Lord Melbourne, as co-respondent. This suit was not successful. But she was, later, widely accused of having sold to *The Times* the secret confided to her by Sidney Herbert, one of her most ardent admirers, of Sir Robert Peel's sudden determination to repeal the Corn Laws. After *Diana of the Crossways* had been published the question of Caroline Norton's responsibility for the disastrous premature disclosure of that political secret was inquired into, and the charge was proved to be false. In view of that inquiry Meredith prefaced the 1890 and subsequent editions of his book with the note ' A lady of distinction for wit and beauty, the daughter of an illustrious Irish house, came under the shadow of a calumny. It has lately been examined and exposed as baseless. The story of *Diana of the Crossways* is to be read as fiction '.

Diana of the Crossways remained, for a considerable period, the most popular of George Meredith's novels. That it should at any time have been the most highly valued by Meredith's genuine admirers is difficult to

credit ; though for its general popularity the main
reason has already been given, and, further, in its
treatment of relation between the sexes, it is more
conventional and less profound than Meredith's other
novels. When the story opens Diana is nineteen—
beautiful, and with already a great reputation for wit.
We see her first at a Dublin ball, in company with an
old General of great distinction, who says of her,
' She makes everything in the room dust around a
blazing jewel.' Here she meets her childhood's friend,
Lady Dunstane, who, with her husband, Sir Lukin,
has been in the General's suite in India. The Dun-
stanes introduce a Mr. Redworth to Diana. He falls
straightway in love with her, but, being practical,
begins to calculate whether he has enough income to
support this bird of Paradise, and decides he has not.
Diana starts on a round of visits ; but her beauty
causes her to be everywhere subject to unwelcome
attentions ; even at Copsley, when she is visiting
Emma Dunstane, the inflammable Sir Lukin has to
be rebuked by her. She leaves that house, and soon
after writes to tell Lady Dunstane of her engagement
to be married to a certain Mr. Warwick. Emma
Dunstane suspects her of having rushed into a loveless
match. Meanwhile Mr. Redworth's speculations in
railways have been prospering, and, at the moment
of Diana's announcement, he finds himself in a
position to have provided for her adequately.
Presently Mr. and Mrs. Warwick arrive on a visit to
Copsley ; Warwick is a ' gentlemanly official ' without
sense of humour, and Lady Dunstane finds herself
wholly unable to account for the marriage. Before

long there come rumours of dissension, and Diana's
name is being coupled with that of the elderly Lord
Dannisburgh, an eminent member of the English
Cabinet. This friendship is known to have been
encouraged by Mr. Warwick for the sake of its
worldly advantages ; but he is jealous, and Diana is
reckless. He takes legal proceedings for a divorce,
and Diana, longing to be free, prepares to leave
England. Lady Dunstane, by her emissary Mr. Redworth, intercepts her at the Crossways, her Sussex
home, and persuades her to face the prosecution.
The suit comes on and is dismissed ; the plaintiff has
not proved his charge. But then there are signs that
Mr. Warwick is about to put the law in motion to
reclaim his wife. To avoid his advances, Diana travels
with some friends. On the Nile she meets the
Hon. Percy Dacier, a nephew of Lord Dannisburgh
and a rising politician. Mr. Redworth, who is now in
Parliament, joins their party for a time. At Rovio,
later in the year, she and Percy Dacier, in an early
morning on the mountains, come within sight of
a passion new in the lives of both of them. On her
return to London, Diana begins novel-writing. Her
first book runs through many editions ; on the
strength of it she sets up an extravagant establishment
and shines as a hostess ; her dinner parties, at which
Percy Dacier is a constant guest, are famous for wit
and wine. Lord Dannisburgh dies ; Diana, in fulfilment of his wish, watches for a night beside his body,
and is joined during her vigil by Percy Dacier. The
name of the beautiful Mrs. Warwick is once more in
the gossips' mouths, and when the hero of Diana's

second novel, *The Young Minister of State*, is recognized as Mr. Dacier, tongues begin to wag about the
friendship between him and the authoress. She is
disappointed in the pecuniary results of the book (the
success of the first was due mainly to Mr. Redworth's
advertisement of it) ; she is living far beyond her
income, and begins to speculate wildly. Mr. Warwick
is said to be dying : to escape his deputed solicitations
Diana goes to a little French watering-place near
Caen. She is followed by Percy Dacier, who now
openly declares his passion for her. She checks him,
and forces him to consider the scandal his visit may
occasion ; but his declaration has revealed to her her
own feelings. She returns to London, and sets to work
upon a third novel, but her financial entanglements
are bewildering. Perfect dinners are swamping her
income. Dacier comes to her constantly for counsel ;
she becomes his right hand in his work ; she believes
that she has her feelings under control. Dacier hears
that Mr. Warwick is actually taking legal proceedings
to secure the return to him of his wife. He comes to
Diana, and begs her to throw in her lot with his : he
is sure of her love. She agrees to meet him, and start
the following evening for France. Her boxes are at
the door when Mr. Redworth appears, and tells her
she must come with him at once to Lady Dunstane,
whose life is in danger. Dacier waits at the station,
sure of Diana. Till within a few minutes of the
starting of the train his confidence does not waver.
The train starts, and he has been fooled. On inquiry
at Diana's house he learns the cause of her absence.
He follows her to Copsley, but no allusion is made by

either to the foiled project. When Emma Dunstane
recovers, Diana makes full confession of it to her.
After some time Diana returns to London and
attempts to take up her old literary life. She and
Dacier meet on their former terms of good-fellowship :
his admiration for her is greater than ever. Redworth
watches their friendship clear-eyed : he thinks well of
Dacier. After one of Diana's most brilliant social
evenings, Percy Dacier returns to her late and alone.
He has ostensibly come to confide to her a great
political secret which will not be published for a
month. Diana is excited by the news : Dacier seizes
his moment and embraces her. She keenly resents the
liberty he has taken and upbraids him. He attempts
to win her consent to a date for their union ; he leaves
her smarting with a sense of dignity lost. Mr. Tonans,
a famous newspaper editor, has sometimes taunted
Diana with over-estimating her knowledge of political
intrigue. She is in urgent need of money. She sells
her secret to Tonans. Dacier has gone home in a whirl
of rapturous feeling. He wakes in the morning to read
his chief's confidence in the daily paper. And he has
been trusted, and no other. They must have been
overheard. In bewilderment he goes to Diana. She
has sold the secret without being aware that it was of
any value ! Dacier leaves her, and shuts the door on
his connexion with Diana. ' To her it was the
plucking of life out of her breast.' Dacier's reflections
cause him to engage himself the same day to
Miss Asper, an heiress who has been piously constant
to him. Diana's husband dies two days before that
marriage. Under the blow of Dacier's desertion,

Diana has herself come near to death. Emma Dunstane wins her back to life and to a renewal of her
former interests. Redworth has never faltered in
feeling : ' He believed in the soul of Diana.' She
rewards him for his long, patient waiting by giving
him her hand.

It is necessary to recapitulate these main events
of the story as basis for comment. In enumerating
them it would have been as little to the point to
include Meredith's elaboration of them as my own
criticism. I may now clear my ground by putting on
record an interpretation of Diana's story, which, if
obviously extravagant, must at least arrest attention
by its originality. An ardent Meredithian exists who
believes that he and Meredith alone had the key to
the story. Diana, he says, is the feminine Egoist ;
and, with a subtlety never for one moment approached
in the book of that name, she is painted as such
without a flaw. By this criticism the artist's work is
revealed less in its intention than in its result. Diana
is brilliant, but can it be denied that she is self-
centred ? The object of her marriage with Mr. Warwick was to escape from unpleasant attentions : it is
not suggested that she loved him. After his lawsuit
it is natural she should object to return to him ; but
what sign does she show of being able to forgo
conventional advantages ? She begins, after a brief
trial of life in lodgings, to entertain lavishly and make
herself the centre of a circle. It is not necessary to
dwell at length here upon Meredith's views as to the
right relation between effort and expenditure ; but
Diana, his favourite, oversteps the limits of her income

from the first, and is represented as largely employed in juggling with debit and credit. When Dacier asks what possible object she could have had in selling him to Tonans, she pleads her dire need of money. Does Meredith really intend us to think that a woman of Diana's intellect could have placed the friend, in whose interests she was entertaining, in such a position? Here we touch the central falsity of the tale. We are not concerned in discussing whether Diana would have been right or wrong to go away with Dacier. The point is, she was saved fortuitously from carrying out that intention. At their next meeting Meredith adroitly takes advantage of the fact that Emma Dunstane is in danger of her life; it is right, at such a moment, that her friend's plans should recede into the background. But what is not right is that Diana should have made confession to Emma of her salvation from sin, and assume, on her return to Dacier, a superiority to which no action of her own has entitled her. It is at least a proof of Dacier's love, which Meredith would represent as worthless, that he reinstates Diana in his regard, and esteems her even more highly than before his humiliation. And now we come to the point at which Meredith attempts to justify his heroine. He has laid much stress on the beauty of Diana's aloofness. He suggests that Dacier returns late at night with his great political news, half in the hope that her excitement may break down her defences. He tells his news and pleads his right to a caress; he gives it unallowed. 'They were speechless. " You see, Tony, my dearest, I am flesh and blood after all." " You drive me to be ice and

door-bolts ! " Her eyes broke over him reproachfully.
" It is not so much to grant," he murmured. " It
changes everything between us." " Not me. It
binds me the faster." " It makes me a loathsome
hypocrite." " But, Tony ! is it so much ? " " Not
if you value it low." " But how long do you keep
me in this rag-puppet's state of suspension ? "
" Patience." " Dangling and swinging day and
night ! " " The rag-puppet shall be animated and
repaid if I have life. I wish to respect my hero.
Have a little mercy. Our day will come ; perhaps as
wonderfully as this wonderful news. My friend, drop
your hands. Have you forgotten who I am ? I want
to think, Percy ! " " But you are mine." " You are
abusing your own." " No, by heaven ! " " Worse,
dear friend ; you are lowering yourself to the woman
who loves you." " You must imagine me superhuman." " I worship you—or did." " Be reasonable,
Tony. What harm ? Surely a trifle of recompense ?
Just to let me feel I live ! You own you love me.
Then I am your lover." " My dear friend Percy,
when I have consented to be your paramour, this kind
of treatment of me will not want apologies."' Is it not
difficult to adopt the position Meredith requires in this
matter, in regard to a woman who has never gone back
on her consent to an immediate and lifelong alliance
with the man she is addressing ? Diana's husband is
dying and any forcing of a new marriage relationship
at the moment is naturally repugnant to her. But it is
hard to see how morality or good taste can so suddenly
be called into question. Consideration of the former,
would have necessitated a clear statement from Diana

as to her error in the past and her ideas for the future ;
the latter, a modification of her public intimacy with
Dacier.   Moreover Dacier's fault should be viewed in
the light of the emotional strain to which Diana had
been subjecting him.   Meredith's suggestion of
grossness in his action is surely the flimsiest of
excuses for Diana's subsequent betrayal.

In regard to the actual betrayal of the secret,
I am far from suggesting that it is an incident which
Meredith might not have incorporated convincingly.
But, in its context, it destroys the foundation on
which his structure has been reared.   It has been
Meredith's contention throughout that Diana's powers
and intellect are exceptional, that uncongenial marriage
restraints and the barriers of conventional routine are
intolerable where she is concerned.   He would have us
believe that she is capable of desiring comradeship
rather than love-making.   A lover comes to her,
believing in her power to appreciate political issues,
and confides to her a secret of great national importance.   (I am not now concerned with the purity of
Dacier's motives, but merely with Diana's capacity
to understand the nature of the gift he has brought.)
She uses it as a trinket to be toyed with and sold.
There are moments indeed when, in comparing the
thirty-first chapter, ' Political News,' with the thirty-
fourth, we are tempted to believe the latter a practical
joke, not excluding its title, ' How the Criminal's
Judge may be Love's Criminal.'   Set side by side with
each other, the discrepancies between Diana's statements, made but twenty-four hours apart, are too
much of a strain on the reader.   In the first scene she

exclaims : ' " And you were charged with the secret all the evening and betrayed not a sign ! . . . The proposal is ? No more compromises ! " " Total ! " Diana clapped hands ; and her aspect of enthusiasm was intoxicating. . . . " We two are a month in advance of all England. . . ." ' In the second she pleads : ' " You did not name it as a secret. I did not imagine it to be a secret of immense *immediate* importance." ' And in reply to his amazed shout of ' What ? ' goes on to say : ' " I had not a suspicion of mischief. . . . I thought it was a secret of a day. I don't think you— no, you did not tell me to keep it secret. A word from you would have been enough. I was in ex-tremity ! " Step by step she recedes before Dacier's interrogation : " I did not imagine he would use it— make use of it—as he has done. . . . No exact sum was named ; thousands were hinted." ' May we not fairly demand of our author a choice between two alternatives ? Either Diana is a fool, passing even the ' ordinary woman ' in her folly (she can entertain the idea of being paid thousands of pounds for information of negligible importance), or she is proving beyond all dispute that the political basis of her intercourse with Dacier is a sham. Diana, Meredith admits, has made a mistake ; but he harps on the insufficiency of her lover's affection, and when Dacier goes out and closes the door on Diana—turns from her intensity to Constance Asper's glacial fidelity—we are given to understand that his error in the eyes of his author is unforgivable. Worldly-wise and narrow-minded Dacier certainly was, but why should this experience with Diana Warwick be

expected to have enlarged his horizon ? Reversion to
Constance Asper appears the natural outcome of it.

It need not be said, since Diana is a Celt and one of
her author's favourites, that she is a mouthpiece for
much of Meredith's wisdom. Her sallies deserve the
fullest quotation ; the Introductory chapter alone is
a treasure-house of wit and of wisdom. But it has
seemed best to set aside in this summary all considerations not bearing on the consistency of the plot.
It is clear, of course, that Meredith means us, as I
suggested in an earlier chapter, to conceive of his
heroine as Redworth conceives of her : ' Redworth
believed in the soul of Diana. For him it burned, and
it was a celestial radiance about her, unquenched by
her shifting fortunes, her wilfulness, and, it might be,
errors. She was a woman and weak ; that is, not
trained for strength. She was a soul ; therefore
perpetually pointing to growth in purification.' This
is what is intended, but is it what is achieved ? I
think not. The events and the psychology of the book
seem to me not only not interwoven, but spun of
materials so different in texture that they could not
combine. The historical figure Meredith chose for his
heroine had a rent in her dress. Every machine in his
factory is set in motion to provide a patch for it. But
the new brocade, compounded of philosophical
speculation and championship of wider opportunities
for women, is a misfit ; ' the rent is made worse.'

Diana's charming personality, her recklessness, her
passion for Dacier, her life-history, including the selling
of the secret, were elements well within Meredith's
power to combine without injuring our love for his

heroine. But, to this end, the reader should have been caught by the heart, not by the head. To start, and to continue to harp, on the note of Diana's wit, her scorn of sentiment and sentimental romance, her clear vision of the failings of her sex, her political views—in short, her philosophy—was to set a tune with which the historical, or supposedly historical, incidents could not be harmonized.

All this, clear enough no doubt to Meredith himself for he writes in March and May 1884 of his great difficulty in winding off this story, would not be worth dwelling upon did it not afford striking support to his own statement that praises and pay from the English public of his time were not accorded to the best of his writings.

Moreover, when *Diana of the Crossways* was succeeding beyond all expectations, its author's thoughts were elsewhere. In June 1884 Mrs. George Meredith underwent a serious operation in a London nursing-home ; another such operation had to take place in January 1885 ; through the following summer she was terribly ill in London and at Eastbourne ; and on the 17th of September 1885 she died at Box Hill.

CHAPTER XI

POEMS OF THE EIGHTIES

MRS. MEREDITH'S painful illness had, in spite of the fortitude with which she had borne it, weighed heavily on her children ; and her death left them both in much need of rest and change. Will, almost immediately after her funeral, went to visit his uncles in Normandy, and Marie, for a time, to the care of Mrs. John Morley in Wimbledon.[1] Meredith retired more than ever into his chalet, even, for a while unfruitfully, into himself ; ' I am,' he wrote to John Morley on New Year's Day 1886, ' still at my questions with death, and the many pictures of the dear soul's months of anguish. When the time was, and even shortly after, I was in arms, and had at least the practical philosophy given to us face to face with our enemy. Now I have sunk, am haunted.' In the summer of that year (1886) he gave courteous welcome to his old friend Sir Francis Burnand, and to Thomas Hardy, at the cottage, where now his Marie was living again with a governess ; and, in August, R. L. Stevenson and Mrs. Stevenson stayed with him there for four days. Yet, for a couple of years at least after the 17th September 1885, the real man was absorbed in that annealing of personal experience from which part of *Ballads and Poems of Tragic Life* and the whole of *A Reading of Earth*, was to result. *A Faith on Trial* and *Change in Recurrence* indeed give

---

[1] *Letters of George Meredith*, vol. ii, p. 373.

to us, with an incisiveness of emotion impossible to
the blunter instrument of realistic description, the
nature and progress of their writer's ordeal at this
date :

> I bowed as a leaf in rain ;
> As a tree when the leaf is shed
> To winds in the season at wane :
> And when from my soul I said,
> May the worm be trampled : smite,
> Sacred Reality ! power
> Filled me to front it aright.
> I had come of my faith's ordeal.[1]

In 1883 Meredith had published *Poems and Lyrics
of the Joy of Earth*. And in his verses which had been
appearing for a number of years before in the *Fortnightly Review* and elsewhere—poems such as *The
Lark Ascending, My Theme, Appreciation, Earth's
Secret*—he, to the eyes of the discerning, had been
making plain his attitude to poetry. That attitude,
much more general to-day than at the time of
George Meredith's writing, carries us back, in a
sense, to early nineteenth-century discussions of the
distinction between Fancy and Imagination. Shortly
described, Meredith's attitude is that, in his writing,
poetry may or may not be attainable ; but that the
one and the only way to it is, not soaring, but the
most careful—meticulously exact—observing and
mapping of footways of this earth, leading, as all of
them did lead to his mind, uphill. Poetry he saw as
the immanence of the spiritual, the poet as the writer
able most truly to observe the real, and, therefore, the

[1] *A Faith on Trial.*

inward, nature of things that *are* seen. To render his meaning to his fellow men, he took the most ordinary, the most prosaic, of words—the word Earth—and poured into it the whole content of his spiritual feeling and experience. ' To understand this word as Meredith understands it ', Mr. Basil de Sélincourt has said, ' is to possess the key to the most secret chambers of his mind ; to think of Earth and feel towards Earth as he does is to be heir to the new inheritance conferred by his poetry upon human life and thought.'

> Not solitarily in fields we find
> Earth's secret open, though one page is there ;
> Her plainest, such as children spell, and share
> With bird and beast ; raised letters for the blind.
> Not where the troubled passions toss the mind,
> In turbid cities, can the key be bare.
> It hangs for those who hither thither fare,
> Close interthreading nature with our kind.
> They, hearing History speak, of what men were,
> And have become, are wise. The gain is great
> In vision and solidity ; it lives.
> Yet at a thought of life apart from her,
> Solidity and vision lose their state ;
> For Earth, that gives the milk, the spirit gives.[1]

As to his method of poetry-writing, *A Reading of Earth* gives us, in a poem called *Outer and Inner*, what is even more of an analysis than an example. The poet is in the woods on a hot August afternoon. Stillness is such that the earth merely breathes. Between him and the heart of Nature so little seems to intervene that his conviction grows stronger than

[1] *Earth's Secret.*

ever that the veil lies over man's eyes only. He
neighbours, indeed he touches, the Invisible. But how
is he to maintain this experience till he can carry back
from it deepened faith and assurance? That is not, as
it would have been to Wordsworth, by soaring through
a perpetuity of rising and setting suns to timelessness
and universality, it is by an exactitude and particularity
of observation that shall insulate him from fancies :

> My world I note *ere fancy comes,*
> Minutest hushed observe.

He indeed, like Wordsworth the crystal-gazer, is
warding off terrestrial reflections ; but he is warding
them off from a burning-glass, not from a globe.
The thread of the spider's noonday spinning, smell of
one kind of leaf, the flies getting up from his path,
each are noted in short-cut words :

> From twig to twig the spider weaves
> At noon his webbing fine.
> So near to mute the zephyrs flute
> That only leaflets dance.
> The sun draws out of hazel leaves
> A smell of woodland wine.
> I wake a swarm to sudden storm
> At any step's advance.
>
> Along my path is bugloss blue,
> The star with fruit in moss ;
> The foxgloves drop from throat to top
> A daily lesser bell.
> The blackest shadow, nurse of dew,
> Has orange skeins across ;
> And keenly red is one thin thread
> That flashing seems to swell.

N

His vision grows even more microscopic, to watch the purposeful comings and goings of the ants in the mosses. And then, when attention is at its minutest and most concentrated, the reward arrives. Not self-induced, nor even preconceived, the new focus has come :

> I neighbour the invisible
>   So close that my consent
> Is only asked for spirits masked
>   To leap from trees and flowers.
> And this because with them I dwell
>   In thought, while calmly bent
> To read the lines dear Earth designs
>   Shall speak her life on ours.

If we consider any of the poems in which George Meredith has gone directly to Nature for his subject, such as *The Lark Ascending*, *The Thrush in February*, *Hard Weather*, *The South-Wester*, *A Night of Frost in May*, we shall perceive that here, in *Outer and Inner*, he has told us his method. Perhaps the most successful, the most consummately successful, achievement of that method is in *The Lark Ascending* :

> He rises and begins to round,
> He drops the silver chain of sound
> Of many links without a break
> In chirrup, whistle, slur and shake,
> All intervolved and spreading wide,
> Like water-dimples down a tide
> Where ripple ripple overcurls
> And eddy into eddy whirls.

We may call this description, for want of a better word ; but if we compare it with Shelley's *Skylark*, for instance, it is as though the lark himself were singing. And this level is sustained, tireless, for sixty lines or more, losing nothing of its force, showering one image after another, all felicitous and some supremely so, leaving the reader at last with the conviction that he never before knew what the lark's song could be—that he has heard it now for the first time. And if he has now heard it, if he has listened to the song indeed, he will, Meredith supposes, be ready to ask and understand what its meaning is and why he delights in it. Briefly, the lark is a fountain overflowing with the joy of life; he is the child of Earth, and whatever is radiant and kindly in the works of Nature is his kin :

> He sings the sap, the quickened veins;
> The wedding song of sun and rains.
> He is, the dance of children, thanks
> Of sowers, shout of primrose banks.

This and much more besides is to be found in him by such as are content to remember that he is still no more than a little feathery bird. A bird he is—no ' spirit '—and a bird he must remain : the gladness and the madness of the poet are different from any-thing he knows. They are at once greater and less. For the lark is indeed all lark, while even the poet is still only half man :

> Was never voice of ours could say
> Our inmost in the sweetest way,
> Like yonder voice aloft, and link
> All hearers in the song they drink.
> Our wisdom speaks from failing blood,
> Our passion is too full in flood,

N 2

> We want the key of his wild note
> Of truthful in a tuneful throat,
> The song seraphically free
> Of taint of personality.

And here is a question raised that cannot be left without an answer. It seems that the lark has a secret that mankind has missed. Who, then, among men comes nearest to the discovery of it? Whom shall we most fitly liken to the lark? To look for him among mere singers would be a superficiality; the resemblance must be sought in some deeper aspect of their common relation to Mother Earth. The value of the lark's song is the wholeheartedness of rapture it expresses, the spontaneous assurance contained in it that life is good. The lark has learned to live according to Earth's ordinance, out of the material Earth has offered him to produce a harmony. The same wholeheartedness of rapture is not yet possible to man; for man has not yet made his life harmonious; but, in the meantime, those men are nearest to the lark's singing who are laying the foundations of a human harmony:

> Whose lives, by many a battle-dint
> Defaced, and grinding wheels on flint,
> Yield substance, though they sing not, sweet
> For song our highest heaven to greet.

These are the true singers, the true soarers; and it is only because here and there he perceives such a one among his fellow men that a poet worthy the name finds himself able to sing at all:

> Wherefore their soul in me, or mine
> Through self forgetfulness divine,

In them, that song aloft maintains,
To fill the sky and thrill the plains
With showerings drawn from human stores.

Thus, finally, the lark ascending grows to a symbol for all human progress. It was by perfectly rendered obedience to natural laws that the lark learned to soar and sing to perfection. Man, who has more complex soaring and singing to learn, cannot learn these in any other way. Once he is in union—in his case conscious union—with Earth's laws, no limit can be set to possibilities of his achievement. As he ascends from an earth entirely understood and fully loved, that earth must widen beneath him illimitably ; for his use and understanding of it

Extends his world at wings and dome
More spacious, making more our home.

It has been necessary, even at the risk of some tedium, thus to follow out the argument of one of Meredith's Nature poems in order to make his method clear. For it might have been imagined at first sight that what he was indicating in *Outer and Inner* as the true attitude of Man to Nature, was merely the ' wise passiveness ' of Wordsworth. It is, indeed, a practice much more conscious and more defined. Meredith repeatedly calls it his ' disciplined habit to see ', and to it he has made, times and again, the greatest sacrifice that it is possible to a poet to make. For it goes without saying that, except an emotional unity is achieved, a true poem cannot exist. Yet, always, when faced with a choice, he has let go the emotional unity rather than sacrifice the fidelity of his

observation. That, of course, is the reason why,
though he is always highly poetic, he only sometimes
in his verse-writing achieves poetry. How great is
the accuracy of Meredith's poetic descriptions is
known to very few persons indeed ; for the simple
reason that very few readers have sufficient knowledge
of the objects that are being looked at in his poems to
be able to estimate the quality of their representation.
To ignorance of the object described, the very clear-
ness of description becomes obscurity. For example,
I may quote the line—of oxen ceaselessly chewing as
they ruminate—' Back to the hours when mind was
mud.' [1] No one who has watched the limitless, un-
applied wisdom that is idiocy, in a cow's eye can
miss the force of that. But, of course, readers exist
who have never looked a cow in the face! Again, there
is that phrase of *Outer and Inner* :

> The foxgloves drop from throat to top
>   A daily lesser bell ; [2]

felicitous as it is, what would it mean in a land where
foxgloves were not known ? And, best of all perhaps
as example of my point, there are the lines describing
what may be called the ' passage work '—the more
troubled and yet less vital, less melodious, parts of the
song of the nightingale—

> There chimed a bubbled underbrew
> With witch-wild spray of vocal dew.[3]

Yet on ears that have not attended to the variations

---

[1] *The Woods of Westermain.*
[2] *Outer and Inner.*
[3] *A Night of Frost in May.*

of that song the exquisite suggestiveness—of bubbling, suppressed, yet spraying, liquidity of sound—is lost. Many illustrations of this sort might be advanced. *The South-Wester* is, notably, another poem in which the high force, its intelligibility even in parts, depends on the extent to which the reader has shared in the observations upon which it is built. But there can be no object in multiplying examples here beyond the point necessary to assure the reader that, when the level of poetry is not attained in Meredith's verse, this is not because the poetic level, as ordinarily accepted among poets and critics, was beyond his reach. On the contrary, we have only to turn to the reviews of his earliest volume of poems to find his work pronounced by some eminent critics as simple, sensuous, and passionate. W. M. Rossetti devoted much of an article on the 1851 *Poems* to making clear to his readers that differences existed between the poetry of Meredith and the poetry of Keats! and Swinburne's admiring phrase 'such passionate and various beauty' I have quoted already in this essay.[1]

Meredith's maturer verse is less emotional only because his mature thought determinedly made passion a servant and not a master. His ideal, in later life, was that the poet must be the philosopher and the philosopher the poet. The final fact about man's emotional capacity, to his view, was its power to make the soul feel itself to be related to truth, its pushing of the individual from his dugout to capture and set upon his intellectual map pieces of

[1] In Chapter IV.

the No-Man's-Land lying between sensation and thought. But how, it may be questioned, did this attitude of Meredith's differ from Blake's attitude out of which came the *Prophetic Books* ? Exactly by the difference of that initial method which I have been trying to describe. Meredith wrote, as late as 1907, to thank a correspondent for asking him what, in the *Hymn to Colour*, was the meaning of :

> By this the dark-winged planet, raying wide,
> From the mild pearl-glow to the rose upborne,
> Drew in his fires, less faint than far descried,
> Pure-fronted on a stronger wave of morn.

' If', Meredith replied, 'you observe the planet Venus at the hour when the dawn does no more than give an intimation, she is full of silver and darkness surrounds her. So she seems to me to fly on dark wings. The image will come home more to you by looking at her ; explanations barely present it. " Black star " is common in classic poets. It is true I push the epithet farther. But so I saw it.' That is, at a moment of supreme rapture, at height of his most sublime allegory of Life and Death and Love, Meredith is not, Blake-like, requiring his reader to become an initiate or user of a glossary, he is still relying on his ' disciplined habit to see ', basing the topmost peaks of his spiritual vision on observation of natural objects that are as open to the ploughboy as they are to himself.

Of course the final achievement poetically, the achievement at which Meredith aimed, is union of complete accuracy of focus with sustained emotional exaltation. In parts of his long poems, such as the passage that begins ' This gift of penetration and embrace ' in *The Test of Manhood*, and ' Thou, of the Highest, the unwritten Law ' in the *Ode to the Comic Spirit*, that combination is achieved. In some number of short poems, such as a *Ballad of Past Meridian*, it is reached and maintained flawlessly. And in the *Hymn to Colour* we have an example of the achievement of the ideal which may suffice us here, both for vindication of the poet, and for test of the reader's capacity to perceive what is offered. For in that—splendid spiritual allegory as it is—there exists hardly a line that does not recall with exactitude some feature or quality of the dawn of half the days of the calendar :

Look now where Colour, the soul's bridegroom, makes
The house of heaven splendid for the bride.
To him as leaps a fountain she awakes,
In knotting arms, yet boundless : him beside,
She holds the flower to heaven, and by his power
    Brings heaven to the flower.

He gives her homeliness in desert air,
And sovereignty in spaciousness ; he leads
Through widening chambers of surprise to where
Throbs rapture near an end that aye recedes,
Because his touch is infinite and lends
    A yonder to all ends.

. . . .

Love eyed his rosy memories : he sang :
O bloom of dawn, breathed up from the gold sheaf
Held springing beneath Orient ! that dost hang
The space of dewdrops running over leaf ;
Thy fleetingness is bigger in the ghost
    Than Time with all his host !

Of thee to say behold, has said adieu :
But love remembers how the sky was green,
And how the grasses glimmered lightest blue ;
How saint-like grey took fervour : how the screen
Of cloud grew violet ; how thy moment came
    Between a blush and flame.

Love saw the emissary eglantine
Break wave round thy white feet above the gloom ;
Lay finger on thy star ; thy raiment line
With cherub wing and limb ; wed thy soft bloom,
Gold-quivering like sunrays in thistle-down,
    Earth under rolling brown.

This indeed is the sunrise as Love perceives it ; it is Nature not seen through a glass darkly, but revealed to poetic vision ' face to face '.

In what is commonly spoken of as the craft of poetry—in metrical and rhythmical experiment—Meredith all his life had been interested. In June of 1868 he had written a notice of ' Robert Lytton's Poems ', extending to fifteen pages of the *Fortnightly Review*, which was practically an essay upon verse-writing. In this he lays down the law that there should not ever, in any poet, be the *habit* of lyrical composition. ' A large and noble theme ', he says, ' has a framework which yields as much support as it demands. Lyrics yield none ; and when they are not spontaneous they rob us of a great deal of our strength and sincerity. If they are true things coming of a man's soul, they are so much taken from him ; if the reverse, they hurry him. A great lyrist (and we have one among us) inflamed by the woes of an un-happy people throbbing for fulness of life and freedom, sings perforce, but he has a great subject, and we do not see that it is his will that distinctly predominates in his verses. Shelley's lyrical pieces are few, considering the vigour of his gift of song ; and so are those of Burns and of Campbell and Hood. Heinrich Heine added a new element to his songs and ballads ; an irritant exile breathed irony into them and shaped them into general form and significance. He is the unique example of a man who made himself his constant theme, and he pursued it up to the time he was rescued from his mattress grave. By virtue of a cunning art he caused it to be interesting while he lived. I feel the monotony of it begin to grow on me often now when I take up the *Buch der Lieder*, the *Neuer Frühling*, and the *Romanzero*. Goethe's songs were the fruit of a long life. He tells us how they sprang up in him, and I do not doubt of his singing as the birds sing ; but without irreverence it may be said that in many cases this was merely a self-indulgent mood to which German verse allured the highest of German poets. I love the larger number of them for his sake, not for their own. The Tuscan Giusti, one of the finest of modern lyrists, published very little. Alfred de Musset's songs, all of them exquisite, might be comprised in half a dozen pages of this review.' In regard to Tennyson's lyrics, just what they achieve and what they miss, Meredith's letters later in his life contain some penetrating observations. The songs of ' Queen Mary ', he wrote, would serve for the ' crisp, salient, excellent ' prose of that work ' if we had not Shakespeare's to show what are not literary forcings to point a com-

parison '.[1]   The best known, though not by any means
the most perfect, of Meredith's own lyrics is *Love
in the Valley*, published in the form in which it now
stands in 1878.   In that, an ordinarily tripping, or at
any rate a samely flowing, regular rhythm

Únder yónder béech-tree síngle ón the gréen-sward

is converted to a delicate melody by intricate ex-
pedients.   Tiny pebbles are inserted in the stream
to ripple its monotony.   For, rightly to scan the lines
of this poem, we must grasp that, in addition to the
ordinary long and short, accented or unaccented,
syllables, we have to deal also with a long accented
syllable equivalent in value to the normal long and
short combined ; that is, the measure being trochaic,
we are liable at any point in the line to have the
trochee replaced by a single long accented syllable.
Very significant, very exquisite also, are the effects
thus obtained.   In

Large and smoky red the sún's cóld dísk dróps

Meredith uses four in succession, droppingly.   In

Úp lánes, wóods thróugh, they troop in joyful bands

he does the same, ascendingly, at the beginning of
a line.   In

Streaming like the flág-réed Sóuth-Wést blówn

---

[1] Of Tennyson's *Idylls of the King* in 1869 Meredith had
written to Maxse, ' The lines are satin lengths, the figures Sevres
china.   I have not the courage to offer to review it, I should say
such things.   To think !—it 's in these days that the foremost
poet of the country goes on fluting of creatures that have not
a breath of vital humanity in them, *and doles out his regular five
feet with the old trick of the vowel endings.*'

we have five carrying us in triumph to the poem's conclusion. And the high success of these lines is in the fact that the accent imposes itself. The reader is, of course, needed to be alert to the degree of stress, but, to sympathetic intelligence, there can be no question where the stresses are to come. At times, indeed, in his poems Meredith seems almost too con-scious of rhythm, too much of an artificer. Certainly, from the days of his 1851 hexameters onward, he did experiment a great deal, and consciously, in verse forms. Of Phaéthôn, written in 1867, he tells us himself ' A perfect conquest of the measure (the galliambic measure) is not possible in our tongue. For the sake of an occasional success in the velocity, sweep, volume of the line, it seems worth an effort ; and, if to some degree serviceable for narra-tive verse, it is *one of the exercises of a writer which readers may be invited to share.*' But there are a number of his poems in which the complexities of his mechanism are so controlled as to afford us something beyond spontaneity—the essence of what is being spoken of, winged, softly close to us for a moment, on words :

> O briar scents, on yon wet wing
> Of warm South-west wind brushing by.

> Sweet as Eden is the air
>   And Eden-sweet the ray.
> No paradise is lost for them
> Who foot by branching root and stem,
> And lightly with the woodland share
> The change of night and day . . .

> For love we Earth, then serve we all ;
> Her mystic secret then is ours :
> We fall, or view our treasures fall,
> Unclouded, as beholds her flowers
>
> Earth, from a night of frosty wreck,
> Enrobed in morning's mounted fire,
> When lowly, with a broken neck,
> The crocus lays her cheek to mire.

> I turned and looked on heaven awhile, where now
> The moor-faced sunset broadened with red light ;
> Threw high aloft a golden bough
> And seemed the desert of the night
> Far down with mellow orchards to endow.

The last of these four extracts makes for us the
transition from lyric to narrative. And it is in his
power of perfectly and indissolubly wedding metre
and descriptive story that George Meredith's peculiar
contribution to English poetry largely consists. In
this respect, passage after passage of *Modern Love*
shows a mastery beyond praise. There is :

> My tears are on thee, that have rarely dropped
> As balm for any bitter wound of mine :
> My breast will open for thee at a sign !
> But, no, we are two reed-pipes coarsely stopped ;
> The God once filled them with his mellow breath :
> And they were music till he flung them down,
> Used ! Used ! Hear now the discord-loving clown
> Puff his gross spirit in them, worse than death.

And there is the opening stanza of *The Day of the
Daughter of Hades*, which one finds oneself repeating
aloud as much for its tangible, what painters would
call its tactile, values as for the sense of its words :

He who has looked upon Earth
Deeper than flower and fruit,
Losing some hue of his mirth,
As the tree striking rock at the root,
Unto him shall the marvellous tale
Of Callistes more humanly come
With the touch on his breast than a hail
From the markets that hum.

Have we not here spontaneity like a bird's, with a man-of-the-law's inevitability of meaning? Through the whole stanza punctuation is unnecessary.

CHAPTER XII

ONE OF OUR CONQUERORS; THE SAGE ENAMOURED AND THE HONEST LADY; 1889–1892

AT the beginning of 1889 Arthur Meredith's health was pronounced broken, and he was started on a voyage to Australia. On the 8th of that February George Meredith wrote to Mrs. Edith Clarke (Edith Nicolls that had been) entreating her to use her influence with her half-brother to persuade him to accept, from his father, some help towards the expense of this travel. 'Tell him', George Meredith writes, 'that I now receive money from America—and there is promise of increase.' Of *Diana of the Crossways* there had been, in America, two pirated editions. Then when in 1885 there had come out in England the first *Collected Edition of Meredith's Novels*, that had been issued, simultaneously, in the United States by Messrs. Roberts of Boston. Now, in 1889, Messrs. Roberts were issuing, again simultaneously with Chapman and Hall in England, the *New* (and cheaper), *Collected Edition*. Moreover, the summer of 1887 had brought to Meredith the news, more valuable to him than any reviewers' acclamations, that the young men of Harvard University were reading, and enthusiastically appreciating, his works.

One of our Conquerors, when it began to appear in the *Fortnightly Review* in October of 1890, was, at the same time, appearing in *The Sun* of New York. Among the greatest of Meredith's novels, *One of our Conquerors* is the most exasperating; its author's mania for metaphor riots in it. Possibly Meredith, as I hinted in writing of *Rhoda Fleming*, has here attempted an impossibility in treating Society— Public Opinion—as a character; the Radnors' visitors presenting too many facets to be synthesized by the reader. Colney Durance and Simeon Fenellan contribute little to the story, while other persons, such as Skepsey, Priscilla, and Mr. Pempton, divert its force by the space they occupy. Yet the book contains some of the most moving scenes in Meredith's work. And, throughout, it is a masterly study of social forces and their wrecking of a man who would, at once, ignore them and have them on his side.

' We are distracted, perverted, made strangers to ourselves by a false position '; this, of Nataly, is the keynote of the book. That fall of Victor Radnor's on London Bridge—the description of which has been a stumbling-block to many—sets us at once on the track of the central idea of his character. How subtle is the would-be *bonhomie* of his recovery, with its instant reinstatement of the Victor he knows, only to be overturned again by sight of smudges on his waistcoat, and by an artisan's misunderstanding of his character! That epitomizes his position in the world. The Radnors, we are to learn, ' walk on a plank across chasms,' but Victor's equilibrium is as a rule so successfully preserved, that he is wont to regard it as the pattern of stability in a world of fluctuations. It is impossible to miss the glamour

of the man, spite of the fact that he is tricked out
in his author's most fantastic vocabulary. In his
actions and effects upon others, he is entirely convincing ; and he is finally drawn and put before us
in his daughter's feeling of his charm, the inspiriting
quality that rushes others, just as it rushes himself,
past criticism or doubt : ' There is no grasping of
one who quickens us.' Everything that Victor puts
his hand to is successful ; wherever he is, he rises
head and shoulders above his comrades. The error
on which he is to be shipwrecked is of no obvious kind.
' Victor had yet to learn that the man with a material
object in aim is the man of his object ; and the nearer
to his mark, often the further he is from a sober
self : he is more the arrow to his bow than the bow
to his arrow. This we pay for scheming : and success
is costly ; we find we have pledged the better half
of ourselves to clutch it ; not to be redeemed with
the whole handful of our prize.' ' He is more the
arrow to his bow than the bow to his arrow ' ; could
Victor's efficiency, covering everything except the
essentials of the situation he is placed in, be better
expressed than in that image ?   He is one of Meredith's triumphs in creation.

The description of Nataly's attitude to Victor is
also consummately successful. She does not dare
analyse him, for that might be to condemn him and
herself—the past through the present. ' And if we
are women, who commonly allow the lead to men,
getting it for themselves only by snaky cunning or
desperate adventure, credulity—the continued trust
in the man—is the alternative of despair.'   That

paints poor tortured Nataly's position; to escape despair she hoodwinks herself, perverts herself, and distracts herself. Meredith has never drawn a more wonderful picture of natural beauty and nobility thwarted, prostrated, twisted, and writhing; beauty and nobility forced to a grimace of pain, and at last almost to ugliness, when she wildly suspects Nesta of not discriminating between herself and the world's Mrs. Marsetts, and touches the worst abyss of false self-scorn. Nataly's position towards Victor, towards Nesta, and towards the world, is the core of the book. The problem is felt mainly through her attitude towards it. With the exception of Chloe, she is the most lovable of Meredith's women—as beautiful and fragile as a flower. Her author has said of her surrender to Victor: ' This might be likened to the detachment of a flower on the river's bank by swell of flood : she had no longer root of her own ; away she sailed, through beautiful scenery, with occasion- ally a crashing fall, a turmoil, emergence from a vortex, and once more the sunny whirling surface ' ; and could the terror in her mind, running as an undercurrent to such sailing, be more completely expressed than in this sentence : ' alarms, throbbing suspicions, like those of old travellers through the haunted forest, where whispers have intensity of meaning, and unseeing we are seen, and unaware awaited ' ? The throb of Nataly's breaking heart and the throb of Victor's ' punctilio bump ' are the *leitmotifs* of the book ; the heart cracking at the end and the brain dissolving. One of the finest chapters is ' Nataly in Action ', a chapter which for beauty, pathos, insight, Meredith has hardly ever surpassed. Nataly's dreamy, feminine thoughts above her anguish in the train, her love of Dartrey sliding insensibly from the maternal to the lover's, till she sees herself in Nesta's place, how beautiful they are ! Apart from its subtlety of drama, that chapter is full of exquisite description. After fainting, ' unreflectingly, she tried her feet to support her, and tottered to the door, touched along to the stairs, and descended them, thinking strangely upon such a sudden weakness of body, when she would no longer have thought herself the weak woman.' How we see her in that ' touched along ' ! Again, ' that doing of the right thing, after a term of paralysis, cowardice—any evil name—is one of the mighty reliefs, equal to happiness, of longer duration ' : and again, when she reaches the station where she is to meet Dudley Sowerby and perform her terrible task, ' Slowness of motion brought her to the plain piece of work she had to do, on a colourless earth, that seemed foggy ; but one could see one's way. Resolution is a form of light, our native light in this dubious world.'

Nesta is less perfectly delineated. In all descriptions of her—smiling, singing, courageously upright, the ' blue butterfly ', or the Britomart, she is attractive, but she is apt to be tiresome in her talk. The episode of Mrs. Marsett is finely contrived to test Nesta and Nataly, to give poor Nataly's heart its most terrible twist (' It 's the disease of a trouble to fly at comparisons ') ; but its significance is over-emphasized, and it is distasteful to see so genuine

and attractive a girl as Nesta showily shoved up into
the saddle of a hobby. But Nesta's love for Dartrey
Fenellan is beautiful, and the silent love scene between
them is one of the great love scenes of literature.

The book abounds in beauty and Meredith's best
wisdom. Dudley Sowerby's mind, in the state of
battle it presents after Nataly's communication, is
admirably portrayed ; ' he had been educated in his
family to believe that the laws governing human
institutions are divine—until History has altered
them. They are altered to present a fresh bulwark
against the infidel.' Was ever a more splendid
landscape painted than in Victor's vision of the
Alps : ' Lo, the Tyrolese limestone crags with livid
peaks and snow lining shelves and veins of the
crevices ; and folds of pine-wood undulations closed
by a shoulder of snow large on the blue ; and a
dazzling pinnacle rising over green pasture-Alps,
the head of it shooting aloft as the blown billow,
high off a broken ridge, and wide-armed in its pure
white shroud beneath ; tranced, but all motion in
immobility, to the heart in the eye ; a splendid
image of striving, up to crowned victory.' And this,
in another vein, is hardly less delightful : ' We are
indebted almost for construction to those who will
define us briefly : we are but scattered leaves to the
general comprehension of us until such a work of
binding and labelling is done. And should the
definition be not so correct as brevity pretends to
make it at one stroke, we are at least rendered
portable ; thus we pass into the conceptions of our
fellows, into the records down to posterity.' Then

there is the portrait of Mr. Barmby, a clerical aspirant
to Nesta's hand : ' he was a worthy man, having
within him the spiritual impulse curiously ready
to take the place where a material disappointment
left vacancy.' And of all these cameos the most
delicate, perhaps, is this of Dudley and Nesta :
' One day, treating of modern Pessimism, he had
draped a cadaverous view of our mortal being in
a quotation of the wisdom of the Philosopher Emperor : " To set one's love upon the swallow is
a futility." And she, weighing it, nodded, and
replied : " May not the pleasure for us remain if we
set our love upon the beauty of the swallow's flight ? " '
Meredith's philosophy is in Nesta's reply.

Almost every current of contemporary ethical
theory was touched on in *One of our Conquerors*—
teetotalism, vegetarianism, simplicity of life, the
place of art in English society, the status of women,
the Salvation Army and its effect on the masses [1]—
these and kindred topics are lengthily discussed. No
one, in fact, who has not read this book can be fully
aware of the keenness, or of the scope, of Meredith's
interests. What may be urged against the book under
this head is that it is a scrap-bag of reflections,
reflections which the fact that they are Meredith's,
and among his best, is not enough to unify. But
the claim of *One of our Conquerors* to greatness rests on
a surer foundation. In the later chapters, at least,
the story is developed with marvellous art. The
subtlest vengeance of social forces has been wreaked

---

[1] It may be of interest to note that *Jump-to-Glory Jane*
appeared in the *Universal Review* in 1890, the year before the
publication of *One of our Conquerors*.

on the Radnors, when Nataly finds herself divided from her child and ranked on the side of convention. And in that closing scene, in the house where Nataly and Victor first met—with its blue satin curtains, its gilt chairs, its Louis Quatorze clock, and Mrs. Berman dying in their midst—how supreme is the art which reveals the colossal spectre that has overhung Nataly and Victor, as a puny woman who has had nothing but her vengeance to support her through the years.

Almost simultaneously with *One of our Conquerors*, *The Sage Enamoured and the Honest Lady* was being produced. It was in the printer's hands in October of 1891. In the previous autumn (the autumn of 1890) Arthur Meredith, who had returned to England from Australia that spring, had died at Mrs. Clarke's house at Woking. On the 6th September he had been buried, and three days later his father had written, to John Morley, ' I pass into the shadow of dear ones, and have to question myself of the kind of lamp I have trimmed to light me. With all the dues to life, I am ready for my day of darkness.' [1] All the dues to life, George Meredith was indeed to render royally to the end ; and the end was not to come for another eighteen and a half years. But, relatively to the earlier glow of his living, he was to be, henceforth, in the shadows. He was now sixty-three years of age, ataxic and apt to be oppressed by the amount he still desired to say within time that necessarily could not now be very long. One of the questions he had felt about most strongly throughout

---

[1] *Letters of George Meredith*, vol. ii, p. 435.

his adult life was the fundamental impurity of the customary masculine identification of ignorance and innocence in women, respecting matters of sex. His *Ballad of Fair Ladies in Revolt*, which he had published as far back as 1876, had, in general terms, tilted inimitably against the 'lily-white' ideal. Now, in *The Sage Enamoured and The Honest Lady* he dared full discussion of the most insistent and unrationalized of all human instincts. In this poem, the Sage, a man of many-sided powers and interests, finds himself drawn to a woman by her graciousness and beauty in a degree that even in his hot-headed youth he should have imagined impossible. The lady reciprocates the feeling sufficiently to find herself constrained to save him from himself—to put an end to his passion. In order to do that, she must tell him the story of her life. She essays that task. But it is not easy. Attempting honest speech, she finds that a mental habit of glossing and clothing compromising facts has affected her choice of words. She wishes the truth to be conveyed, but desires her friend's image of her to be unaffected by it. The picture she sketches is of two young and passionate lovers hurled by outraged society into a yet closer embrace, pledged more deeply to one another by the imminent danger of forced severance. They err, and in the world's eyes are ruined ; but they make their appeal to the Court of Love, and are able to esteem their gain above their loss—

invoke an advocate
In passion's purity, thereby redeemed.

The Sage, her lover, now become her judge, remains mute and unresponsive. He envelops her in an icy silence that freezes her burning plea ; and in her bitterness she sees him as a leader of the male herd stoning the women they abase. But her words reverberate, as it were, in the emptiness, and, hearing them, she recognizes their hollowness.

She no longer glosses her offence, but grasps at its ugliest, its scriptural, title. Thereupon natural repulsion in her hearer gives place to something higher and nobler :

> Crimson currents ran
> From senses up to thoughts,

enabling him to realize in the valiancy of this sacrifice for his enlightenment a flower more delicate than any rosebud of guileless maidenhood, and to grasp something of the need of understanding involved in the effort necessary to such a confession :

> He gave her of the deep well she had sprung ;
> And name it gratitude, the word is poor.
> But name it gratitude, is aught as rare
> From sex to sex ?   And let it have survived
> Their conflict, comes the peace between the pair,
> Unknown to thousands husbanded and wived :
> Unknown to Passion, generous for prey :
> Unknown to Love, too blissful in a truce.
> Their tenderest of self did each one slay ;
> His cloak of dignity, her fleur de luce ;
> Her lily flower, and his abolla cloak,
> Things living, slew they, and no artery bled.
> A moment of some sacrificial smoke
> They passed, and were the dearer for their dead.

The bulk of the poem now deals with the Sage's treatment of the issues raised by the personal situation, to which the story has introduced us. And this method, call it scientific or inartistic if you will, like it or leave it, is eminently characteristic of Meredith's work. Again and again in his novels he looks over his own shoulder, as it were, to comment on his inveterate habit of proceeding from the particular to the general. But in the possibility of so doing he has seen the main claim of the particular upon our attention. His anticipation of criticism in this case takes the form of a statement in regard to the Sage's treatment of his friend :

He passed her through the sermon's dull defile,
and that statement in one sense is an apology. No one, he would say, deplores a tendency to dullness and sermonizing on the part of his characters more deeply than their creator. But the subject under consideration appears to him too profoundly important for the discussion of it to be limited by any claims other than its own. An artistic setting, a certain vitalizing of the problem in particular human experience, was essential to its presentment ; but to limit it to these would be to beg the points of interest, to neglect to draw attention to the elements within it that really are obscure. Meredith's Sage, regrettably, may be dull ; but none the less his claim to the title that he bears is based on his capacity for classifying and relating the experiences of his life to a world that is outside himself, for passing swiftly from purely personal discomfort to a vision of the essential qualities of the tale he has just heard.

Passionate human love, a force that garnered and cherished should have been serviceable for a lifetime, by recklessness has been reduced to :

These few last
Hot quintessential drops of bryony juice,
Squeezed out in anguish : all of that once vast !

Nevertheless he holds no brief for a hypocritical world, preserving its so-called purity at the price of gross injustice, visiting punishment for a joint deed on one only of the participators. There exist two opposing camps in this matter, but neither of them can claim to have reached a solution reconciled with the facts : one lops off a limb, a piece of life itself, the other rebels against the consequences issuing from indulgence of its instincts. By one school Nature is accounted devilish, by the other divine. But the intellectual deadlock reached by both is the same : both

accept for doom
The chasm between our passions and our wits.

It is the old story—Nature misread, taken as synony-mous with the instincts of the flesh, separated from the idealization of the spirit. The only solution is to recognize that man's mind and man's laws, what-ever their crudity, are not alien and opposing products but are, no less than his body, outcome of Nature's chastening discipline ; the one way of escape from individualistic rebellion being to conceive the collective mind of man as ' child of her keen rod ', his earliest laws developing as :

the blind progressive worm
That moves by touch, and thrust of linking rings,[1]

[1] Cf. *The World's Advance.*

his later and more complex aims demanding and
necessitating a deliberate weighing of the present
with the future, the immediate with the remote.
Self-satisfaction, Happiness, there are no more fixed
sources of these than there is a finite, stable compound
of qualities to be termed Human Nature. Man's
conception of pleasure is changing and developing
with his civilization. And wherever he has attempted
to substitute an ideal end for an immediate satisfaction, it follows that he has discerned, afar and
flickering, but still discerned, the beacon of some
higher joy. In a humanity thus developing, many
desires fall away and are superseded. The problem
raised by sexual passion is unique, because, being
the channel of life itself, its continuance is essential.
The question of its ultimate place in society is insistent, and refuses to be shelved or ignored. Clearly,
its blind assertiveness must be checked and controlled by ideals touching the welfare of the race
to be. But how and in what manner ? The answer
must be comprehensive, and to frame it man and
woman :

> the twain beside our vital flood,
> Now on opposing banks, the twain at strife,

must face the problem considerately, and in unison :

> Instruct in deeper than Convenience,
> In higher than the harvest of a year.

To Meredith's mind the Sage's power of abstract
judgement betokens more, and not less, capacity for
sympathy and emotion. The era he has been fore-
seeing, when man and woman shall meet to mate as

peers, has not yet arrived. And meanwhile, in such a situation as the present, abstractedly considered, a tenderness deeper than philanthropy appears to him the

> step to right the loaded scales
> Displaying women shamefully outweighed.

By his fearless treatment of the problem of sex and the long discipline needful to its solution, the Sage has released his companion from the prison-house of her isolation, put her once more into step with her fellows, taught her to hear again the heart-beat of the world. She no longer shrinks from, or slurs over, the fact of her experience ; she accepts it as the road to her awakened understanding of comrade- ship and of law, the groundwork of her new feeling for the tranquil and impersonal :

> The peace, the homely skies, the springs that welled ;
> Love, the large love that folds the multitude.

His own reward is present too, in his quickened and deepened conception of loveliness ; the old outward attraction is still obvious, but it shrinks to insigni- ficance before the beauty of spirit he has apprehended now :

> Soul's chastity in honesty, and this
> With beauty, made the dower to men refused.
> And little do they know the prize they miss ;
> Which is their happy fortune ! Thus he mused.

The prospect open to these lovers is widely different from that of the lady's youthful desires or the Sage's preconception. Not vivid in colour, or striking in

outline, it is strangely fair to view.   No splendid and
triumphant dawn is theirs ; but daybreak on a
quiet day :

> He needed her quick thirst
> For renovated earth : on earth she gazed,
> With humble aim to foot beside the wise.
> Lo, where the eyelashes of night are raised
> Yet lowly over morning's pure grey eyes.

CHAPTER XIII

LORD ORMONT AND HIS AMINTA; THE AMAZING MARRIAGE, 1892–1895

IN the spring of 1893 George Meredith was at work again each day, from 10.30 a.m. to 6 p.m., on a novel, and the novel was *Lord Ormont and his Aminta*.[1] At Box Hill now his family consisted only of himself and his daughter ; in the autumn of 1892 William Maxse Meredith had married a Miss Elliot, of Leith Hill.[2] The father and daughter at this date were closely in touch with, and at times visiting, General Palmer of Colorado and his family, who were then renting Loseley Hall near Guildford. But, in the main, Meredith's days were being given to writing as, with insecure strength, he had now, over and above his writing of *Lord Ormont*, heavily on his mind his agreement with the editor of *Scribner's Magazine* that a novel of his should be ready for that magazine in the following spring.[3]

Lord Ormont and his Aminta is much simpler in style than is *One of our Conquerors*. Its story was suggested to Meredith by the career of the Earl of Peterborough whom Macaulay called ' the last of the knights errant ', and who won wide fame at Valencia but was recalled by his country in 1707,

[1] *Letters of George Meredith*, vol. ii, p. 460.

[2] Miss Meredith was to marry Henry Parkman Sturgis in the summer of 1894.

[3] *Letters of George Meredith*, vol. ii, p. 461. This was to be the last of Meredith's novels—*The Amazing Marriage*.

partly on account of the jealousy of his colleagues
but partly also because of his high-handed temper.
Privately married to the famous singer Anastasia
Robinson about 1733, he for some reason refused to
acknowledge her publicly as his wife till close on
his death a dozen years after. At this novel's appearance, critics tended to dwell with admiration or the
success of a description of a boys' school with which
the tale opens. As to that success there is room for
two opinions. It is not, in any case, a realistic
representation ; but then, neither is the magnificent
swimming scene at the close of the book realistic,
and we must at once allow that, if actuality be
demanded of *Lord Ormont and his Aminta*, the story
will be found to have flaws. Is it, for instance,
credible that Weyburn could have been within Lord
Ormont's house for days without recognizing Aminta ?
Is it possible, even if we accept in this matter
the complete setting aside of her husband's tastes,
that Aminta herself would have continued to bear
with Mrs. Pagnell's vulgarity ? And in regard to
the leading incident of the book, Weyburn's noble
international school rests on the shaky foundation
of a deceit. He and Aminta feel themselves
justified in the step they have taken ; moreover
Aminta's husband is, ultimately, satisfied, if not
actually approving. But all this, though it exonerates
them as individuals, falls wide of the mark so far as
building up the school is concerned. Inevitably,
parents of the boys are to think of Weyburn and
Aminta as married ; and thus, though the righteousness of the pair is eminently arguable, it cannot be

argued with the persons concerned. At the period, and in the social conditions, Meredith is postulating, they would quickly have found themselves in untenable positions.

The living story begins with the description— when Weyburn comes as secretary to Lord Ormont— of Aminta's gaze. There is pathos in this vision of the mysterious lady with the cloud upon her ; and the whole scene, of Weyburn's and Aminta's meeting, is here charmingly conceived ; their, as yet unrecognized, memories breathing through present obscurity. The tale centres in the cloud over Aminta, and Weyburn's growing consciousness of it is very skilfully developed. Smirchings from Lady Charlotte's chatter drop away in Aminta's presence, but the cloud remains. Lord Ormont's position, in respect to that cloud, is only to be understood when the reader realizes that, although the original error was Lord Ormont's, it is as a result of her own actions that Aminta is in the situation in which Weyburn finds her. Lord Ormont, like many other of Meredith's masculine characters, has lost the power of seeing any woman individually, apart from his general notions as to her sex. His attitude to the woman he has taken as his wife, though it differs in degree, does not differ in kind from the attitude he has adopted to others. Yet a happy sidelight on their six years of marriage before the opening of the story is given by their occasional reversions to the old nicknames of ' Xarifa ' and ' Knight Durandarte '. They were married at the Embassy in Madrid (Aminta is partly Spanish), and have roamed about Europe

ever since. Having been censured for high-handed-
ness in his conduct of affairs in India, Lord Ormont
was, and still is, completely at loggerheads with his
country, and consequently at loggerheads also with
his most intimate relation, the one person who is
not to be deceived by his would-be contempt for
England. He is the most gallant of comrades, and
has real love for Aminta ; but the last thing he had
expected her to demand was the dullness and decorum
of conventional English society ; and he has regarded
it as part of the tacit understanding between them,
that she should be included in his self-inflicted
banishment from the land of his birth. But Aminta,
mainly at her aunt's instigation, has now begun to
press for settlement in England and open acknowledgement of her position as Countess of Ormont.
The Earl, hardly more in annoyance than amusement,
sees that to submit to his wife's tactics would involve
coming to terms with his country, and, if the game
of Pull and Pull is to be played, he is ready for his
part in it. When the story opens, Aminta has so
far prevailed that they are living in London ; but
to all her hints and suggestions in regard to Steignton,
the Earl's country seat, he replies imperturbably
that it is let, and that he is well enough satisfied with
his tenant. Aminta's aunt, Mrs. Nargett Pagnell
(her character is to be inferred from her name, and
from her pronunciation of it, Naryett Paynell), is
staying in the house, and daily grows more clamorous
in her effort to secure public acknowledgement for
her niece. Behind this situation, looms Lady Charlotte Eglett, Lord Ormont's sister already referred

to, publicly incredulous of the idea that her brother
has given Aminta his name : into it, Aminta's old
schoolboy lover, and Lord Ormont's adorer, Matey
Weyburn, is precipitated ; and the story moves to
its end.   Aminta is very gracefully drawn ;   her
bewilderment and fluctuations of feeling—the whirl-
pool-sucking to contemplate the dangerous passion
Morsfield offers her, and the sweet sunny contrast of her
love for Weyburn—it is all excellent.   Weyburn, too,
is really a very pleasant fellow, and though Meredith
makes him talk like a prig occasionally, there is no
strain of priggishness in his nature.   The scene by
the deathbed of Weyburn's mother is enriched with
some of the choicest flowers of Meredith's thought.
' His prayer was as a little fountain, not rising high
out of earth, and in the clutch of death ; but its being
it had from death, his love gave it food.'   ' Prayer is
power within us to communicate with the desired
beyond our thirsts.'   ' We do not get to any heaven
by renouncing the mother we spring from ;   and
when there is an eternal secret for us, it is best to
believe that Earth knows, to keep near her, even
in our utmost aspirations.'   And some of the adroitest
of Meredith's sayings, such as of friendship—' If
it is not life's poetry, it is a credible prose ; a land
of low undulations instead of Alps ; beyond the
terrors and deceptions,'—are to be found in the book.
But its power culminates in the two splendid climaxes
—Aminta's flight from Steignton, and the scene in
which, in Lady Charlotte's presence, her farewell
letter reaches Lord Ormont.   In the first, the
description of the country flying by as they drive

is one of Meredith's triumphantly living landscapes ;
the second is among the greatest things he has
written. Meredith seldom appeals to tears ; he does
so here. Owing to Aminta's pursuit by unworthy
admirers, Lord Ormont has been slowly coming to
see that his secrecy as to their marriage has placed
her in an impossible position ; and, without her
knowledge, he is preparing amends on the scale of
his character. After a long and wearisome tussle,
he has at last secured from his sister the family
jewels, which till now she had resolutely refused to
relinquish. Lady Charlotte comes to see him, being
in anxiety about his health. She expresses relief
at his appearance, and alludes to reviving appreciation of his worth. ' " The country wants your
services," she says. " I have heard some talk of it.
That lout comes to a knowledge of his wants too
late. If they promoted and offered me the command
in India to-morrow—" My lord struck the arm of
his chair. " I live at Steignton henceforth : my
wife is at a seaside place eastward. I take her down
to Steignton two days after her return. We entertain
there in the autumn. You come ? " " I don't.
I prefer decent society." " You are in her house
now, ma'am." " If I have to meet the person you
mean, I shall be civil. The society you've given her
I won't meet." " You will have to meet the Countess
of Ormont if you care to meet your brother." " Part
then on the best terms we can. I say this, the woman
who keeps you from serving your country, she 's
your country's enemy." " Hear my answer. The lady
who is my wife has had to suffer from what you call

my country's treatment of me. It 's choice between
my country and her. I give her the rest of my time."
" That 's dotage."   " Fire away your epithets."
" Sheer dotage. I don't deny she 's a handsome
young woman." " You'll have to admit that Lady
Ormont takes her place in our family with the best
we can name."   " You insult my ears, Rowsley."
" The world will say it when it has the honour of her
acquaintance."   " An honour suspiciously deferred."
" That 's between the world and me.". . . Letters of
the morning's post were brought in. The earl turned
over a couple and took up a third, saying : " I'll
attend to you in two minutes," and thinking once
more : Queer world it is where, when you sheathe
the sword, you have to be at play with bodkins.
Lady Charlotte gazed on the carpet, effervescent with
retorts to his last observation, rightly conjecturing
that the letter he selected to read was from " his
Aminta ".' The time seems endless to her befoɪe
his reading is done. Lord Ormont's appearance is
strange. ' " No bad news, Rowsley ? " The earl's
breath fell heavily. Lady Charlotte left her chair
and walked about the room. " Rowsley, I'd like to
hear if I can be of use." " Ma'am," he said, and
pondered on the word " use ", staring at her. " I
don't intend to pry. I can't see my brother look like
that and not ask." The letter was tossed on the
table to her.' She read the lines dated from Felix
stowe. It is final and it is long, dealing with details
of administration and housekeeping, of drawers and
labelled keys, and where the Ormont jewels have
been left. ' " The woman is cool," Lady Charlotte

ejaculated; and, " will she be expecting you to
answer, Rowsley ? "   " Will that forked tongue
cease hissing ! " he shouted, in the agony of a strong
man convulsed, both to render and conceal the
terrible, shameful, unexampled gush of tears. Lady
Charlotte beheld her bleeding giant. She would
rather have seen the brother of her love grimace in
woman's manner than let loose those rolling big
drops down the face of a rock. The big sob shook
him, and she was shaken to dust by the sight. Now
she was advised by her deep affection for her brother
to sit patient and dumb behind shaded eyes. . . .
Neither opened mouth when they separated. She
pressed and kissed a large nerveless hand. Lord
Ormont stood up to bow her forth.' This crumbling
of brother and sister—how touching, how terrible,
it is !

Before going on to speak of the last of Meredith's
novels—*The Amazing Marriage*—this seems the place
to admit that a good deal of the argument of
Diana of the Crossways, Lord Ormont and his Aminta,
and *The Amazing Marriage* is ' dated '. And that
admission is made the more necessary in that my
claim in general is that Meredith's work is concerned
with the eternal, and not the temporary, qualities of
human nature. Women refusing the conditions
which Mr. Warwick, Lord Ormont, and Fleetwood
attempted to impose on their wives could not be
regarded as social rebels in England anywhere to-
day. In every civilized country the position of women
has been, in the past forty years, changing almost
out of recognition, and for that change, in England,

George Meredith more than any other writer was responsible.

Yet the many desirable changes worked in the last forty years in public opinion have brought with them one effect that Meredith would certainly wish to ignore. A type of mind has arisen which, reacting against lifeless constraints, looks on all social convention and contract as tyrannical, and on self-expression as the only necessity. This type has no place in the 'honourable minority' Meredith addresses. In that, a social consciousness, a staunch belief in society, is presumed, in addition of course to personal susceptibilities ; otherwise the possessors of those susceptibilities stand marked, Byronlike, as the Comic Spirit's prey. In other words, if we can see nothing at all to be said for the claims of Mr. Warwick, Lord Ormont, and Fleetwood, if because Diana, Aminta, and Carinthia are superior to their lords, we do not feel they have incurred any obligation by their vows, we are not among those for whom Meredith was writing. The art and the labour he expends to justify his exceptions, presuppose the existence of a rule. At the moment when he asks unconventional action of his characters, its effectiveness depends upon the rarity of its occurrence. 'When we find ', he writes of one of the finest and most lovable of them, ' a man who is commonly of the quickest susceptibility to ridicule as well as to what is befitting, careless of exposure, we may reflect on the truthfulness of feeling by which he is drawn to pass his own guard and come forth in his nakedness.' No problem indeed could exist for

Aminta and Carinthia were it not for their recognition
of a standard that is abstract and non-individual;
and this standard Weyburn, in vowing himself to
Aminta, openly expresses : ' With a world against
us,' he says, ' our love and labour are constantly on
trial ; we must have great hearts, and if the world
is hostile we are not to blame it. In the nature of
things it could not be otherwise. My own soul, we
have to see that we do—though not publicly, not
insolently—offend good citizenship. But we believe—
I with my whole faith, and I may say it of you—that
we are not offending Divine Law. You are the
woman I can help and join with, think whether you
can tell yourself that I am the man. So then our
union gives us power to make amends to the world.'
' Make amends to the world'—the first note, and the
last, is this of good citizenship. This is the Court
of Appeal, the test to which individualistic action
has to be referred. It is significant that practically
the whole of Meredith's later treatment of Weyburn
and Aminta is concerned with their great school and
its striking success.

In creative energy, *The Amazing Marriage* equals
any of its predecessors. The fire of *Sandra Belloni*
unites with the intellectual subtlety of *The Egoist*,
with the result that both are more humane ; neither
claims mastery ; they are content to serve a single
purpose. In details, the old artifices are present ;
the opening chapter is entitled ' Dame Gossip as
Chorus ', and quotations are many from a script
called ' Maxims for Men '. The story does not really
begin till the fourth chapter, where Chillon John

and his sister Carinthia set out, from their Bavarian
home, on a journey to England. Yet the first three
chapters contain much of the great-heartedness of
the Old Buccaneer and the valiant aristocracy of
the woman he so tenderly loved, which presently will
be needed to build up our picture of their daughter
Carinthia. Indeed these prefatory chapters so strongly
affect the after situation, that we shall need to modify
our instinctive view of the part Carinthia's husband
plays in that, by the recollection that we have
knowledge he does not share. Where he thought
confusedly of the Old Buccaneer as one who had
flouted the laws of society, and was therefore, pre-
sumably, of the undisciplined, the reader has been
allowed clear view of one who ' never had failed in an
undertaking without stripping bare to expose himself
where he had been wanting in intention and determination '.

Carinthia belongs with mountains and the dawn.
We see her first on a twelve-foot leap from a window
of her dismantled home, going with her brother
before daybreak to recover their childhood in a game
of ' calling the morning ' from the mountain-top.
Nowhere in his prose descriptions has Meredith
surpassed his picture of dawn as Carinthia and
Chillon saw it that day ; to the heroine of this,
his last, novel he has lent his poetic vision at
its intensest : ' Dawn in the mountain-land is a
meeting of many friends. The pinnacle, the forest-
head, the latschen-tufted mound, rock-bastion and
defiant cliff and giant of the triple peak, were in view,
clearly lined for a common recognition, but all were

figures of solid gloom, unfeatured and bloomless. Another minute and they had flung off their mail and changed to various, indented, intricate, succinct in ridge, scar, and channel; and they had all a look of watchfulness that made them one company. The smell of rock-waters and roots of herb and moss grew keen; air became a wine that raised the breast high to breathe it; an uplifting coolness pervaded the heights. What wonder that the mountain-bred girl should let fly her voice. The natural carol woke an echo. She did not repeat it. "And we will not forget our home, Chillon," she said, touching him gently to comfort some saddened feeling.

'The plumes of cloud now entered slowly into the lofty arch of dawn and melted from brown to purple-black. The upper sky swam with violet; and in a moment each stray cloud-feather was edged with rose, and then suffused. It seemed that the heights fronted East to eye the interflooding of colours, and it was imaginable that all turned to the giant whose forehead first kindled to the sun; a greeting of god and king.

'On the morning of a farewell we fluctuate sharply between the very distant and the close and homely: and even in memory the fluctuation occurs, the grander scene casting us back to the modestly nestling, and that, when it has refreshed us, conjuring imagination to embrace the splendour and wonder. But the wrench of an immediate division from what we love makes the things within reach the dearest, we put out our hands for them, as violently parted lovers do, though the soul in days to come

would know a craving, and imagination flap a leaden
wing, if we had not looked beyond them.

'"Shall we go down?" said Carinthia, for she knew
a little cascade near the house, showering on rock
and fern, and longed to have it round her. They
descended, Chillon saying that they would soon have
the mists rising, and must not delay to start on their
journey.

'The armies of the young sunrise in mountain-lands
neighbouring the plains, vast shadows, were marching
over woods and meads, black against the edge of
golden; and great heights were cut with them, and
bounding waters took the leap in silvery radiance
to gloom; the bright and dark-banded valleys were
like night and morning taking hands down the sweep
of their rivers. Immense was the range of vision
scudding the peaks and over the illimitable Eastward
plains flat to the very East and sources of the sun.'

Changefulness of aspect is one of the resemblances
between Carinthia and her mountain home. Her
brother, scrutinizing her face for some foresight of
her fortune, finds himself fearing she is plain, or at
any rate not handsome, though at times her features
had seemed to him marvellous in animation. Woodseer is to see deeper, but his phrases—'a haggard
Venus,' 'a beautiful Gorgon,'—are too epigrammatic
to serve as descriptions; he is happier in his less
ambitious suggestions of a particular quality that
comes and goes, 'a panting look,' 'a look of beaten
flame,' 'from minute to minute she is the rock that
loses the sun at night and reddens in the morning.'
Fleetwood, on his first meeting with Carinthia, finds

good breeding, and something beyond good breeding, stamped on her features. But it is one of the greatest tributes to Meredith's art that, without any direct statement on his part other than these half-hearted commendations of Carinthia's contemporaries, his readers are in no way astonished by Henrietta's account of Carinthia's appearance at the ducal ball. ' Chillon,' writes Henrietta, ' she was magical! You cannot ever have seen her irradiated with happiness. Her pleasure in the happiness of all around her was part of the charm. One should be a poet to describe her. It would task an artist to paint the rose-crystal she became when threading her way through the groups to be presented. That is not meant to say that she looked beautiful. It was the something above beauty—more unique and impressive—like the Alpine snow-cloak towering up from the flowery slopes you know so well.' By the time age is reached, loveliness of this quality will, to some extent at least, have stamped itself on the features ; but in youth it comes and goes, flaming at its intensest in moments of stress, when some unexpected call for action is made. And it is part of the perfection of Meredith's workmanship in this matter that we are never asked to realize Carinthia's face in quiescence. Our vision of her, after her marriage, lives in two scenes—her parting with her husband on her wedding day, and her final conversation with him a year or two later, in Wales. In the first, Fleetwood, who except on top of the coach has not been alone with her since the ceremony in the church, comes to announce to Carinthia that he is leaving her for an indefinite

period. She has had no preparation for this news.
He finds her in the inn sitting-room. ' She was
seated ; neither crying nor smiling, nor pointedly
serious in any way, not conventionally at her ease
either. . . . She spoke without offence, the simplest
of words, affected no solicitudes, put on no gilt smiles,
wore no reproaches : spoke to him as if it so happened
—he had necessarily a journey to perform. One could
see all the while big drops falling from the wound
within. One could hear it in her voice. Imagine
a crack of the string at the bow's deep stress. Or
imagine the bow paralysed at the moment of deepest
sounding. And yet the voice did not waver. She
had now the richness of tone carrying on a music
through silence. . . . Her brown eyes were tearless,
not alluring or beseeching or repelling ; they did but
look, much like the skies opening high aloof on a
wreck of storm. Her reddish hair—chestnut, if you
will—let fall a skein over one of the rugged brows,
and softened the ruggedness by making it wilder, as
if a great bird were winging across a shoulder of the
mountain ridges. No longer the chalk-quarry face—
its paleness now was that of night Alps beneath
a moon chasing the shadows.' To some of us this
suggestion of a whole by various half-defined,
flickering, images will seem the sole means by which
Meredith could have achieved the end he here has
in view—that end being not the portrayal of a thing
polished and complete, but the adumbration of
a loveliness as yet unrealized. Others will complain
of heaped metaphor, by its very variety rendered
meaningless. But of these last it may fairly be

demanded that they add, to the recollection of what
has already been said of Meredith's use of metaphor
in general, a careful consideration of the task he had
put to himself here.   As in his abstract treatment
of life he moves on the horizon of thought, flashing
gleams from hither and thither on some blurred, and
hitherto meaningless, presence, to set it revealed in
poetry or prose to his fellows for the thing that it
is, so in the heroine of this, his last, novel he has
given presentation and shape to a kind of beauty,
winged and elusive, which, while it hovered on the
borderland of man's consciousness, had, up to this
time, hovered uncaught.[1]

While Chillon and Carinthia are crossing the
mountains to Baden, Gower Woodseer and Lord
Fleetwood, each baulked in his search for solitude,
are making friends on the shores of a neighbouring
lake.   Fleetwood is tied to this district by the presence
there of the beautiful Henrietta Fakenham.   On the
relationship of this strangely assorted pair—the young
man who believed he had achieved a philosophical
outlook at the age of twenty-three, and the young
peer who desired to be more of a dreamer than he
actually was—Meredith has expended his subtlest
powers.   In the tastes of the two there is much in
common ; and their different circumstances afford
the piquancy they require.   Readers familiar with
The Empty Purse will not find it difficult from the
outset to predict that, of these two theorists, he who
replies to the wealthy Lord Fleetwood's ' May I ask

[1] A more or less parallel achievement of our day is in *The
Constant Nymph.*

which of the Universities ? ' with a panegyric of
his schooling on the Open Road and the words ' I
have studied in myself the old animal having his
head pushed into the collar to earn a feed of corn ',
will be the earliest to reach human effectiveness.
Yet, even though the final harbourage of Woodseer's
nature is foreseen, there are signs from the first that
his impressionable personality will be involved in
back-eddies and tides before his anchorage is secure.
For, on the threshold of his story, Meredith's old
danger-signal appears. Woodseer's insight is real,
his penetration undoubted, but he labours under
a disadvantage general in men who have developed
among their intellectual inferiors. Having evolved
certain theories of life for himself, he is unable to hold
them with sufficient relativity, or to grasp the
complexity of the interests against which he inveighs.
Dragons that have slain strong men, he imagines,
may be dismissed in epigrams. He cries scorn at
thought of any possible allurement for him in the
green tables at Baden, or of submission to any
personal attraction not rooted in similarity of ideas.
Consequently, before he leaves the tables, he has
emptied the purse of another as well as his own ; and
in submission to Livia's fascination he betrays the
trust of a dying man. Meredith's comment on the lofty
tone in which Woodseer explains that, being without
money to lose or any inclination to gain, he is free of
all temptation to gambling, is highly characteristic—
' They were,' Meredith says, ' no doubt good reasons
and they were grand morality. They were at the same
time customary phrases of the unfleshed in folly.'

At his first meeting with Fleetwood, Woodseer imagines a high degree of sympathy to exist between them, because of Fleetwood's power of visualizing a face which he has merely read about in Woodseer's diary. Presently, however, a dispute as to the exact phrase by which Carinthia's appearance is best to be described leads to a coolness. That matter is one on which neither of them is prepared to give way; for they are both, in their widely different circumstances, intellectually overweening. Up to this point, and for some time after, notably in his visit to the Carlsruhe tailor, his conduct at the gaming tables, and his adoration of the Countess Livia, Woodseer shows as Lord Fleetwood's inferior—in abstract intellectuality his equal, but from lack of social sense his inferior. Why, and at what stage, then, we may ask, does the young Welshman overtake, and begin to outstrip, his friend? Half through the story Fleetwood himself is astounded to realize that, instead now of idealizing the Countess Livia, Woodseer has not the smallest desire to fall in with his lordship's schemes for their marriage; that he has, in fact, asked and won the love of Carinthia's waiting-maid and friend, a girl in many ways resembling her mistress. Fleetwood possesses enough grace and insight to recognize Woodseer's spiritual progress in these changes; but he is much at a loss to understand how they have occurred. For the reader who has seen the working of Meredith's mind, explanations are not far to seek. Such development is mainly attributable to Woodseer's circumstances—the fact that he has no riches to wall him off from life's teachings. Also, he had an advantage the reverse side of which I have already stated. He has just been seen, from lack of social experience, to take his personal convictions too ponderously. But they are real convictions. He has not toyed with his intellect, or learned to divorce his beliefs from his actions. It was inevitable that his inexperience should have been overpowered by Livia's arts, that, at first, he should have succumbed to temptations that were coupled with her intimacy. What was not inevitable, what is in fact peculiar to men of his kind, 'men with a passion for spiritual cleanliness,' was his power of recognizing, immediately and without prompting, when he had erred. His father speculates in his presence as to what can be the nature of Carinthia's husband, demanding 'Can you imagine the doing of an injury to a woman like her?' and Woodseer replies, 'Yes, I can imagine it, I'm doing it myself. I shall be doing it till I've written a letter and paid a visit.' This confession made, he proceeded at once to the writing of the letter to Fleetwood, undeterred by the facts that his having to intrude his name on that nobleman's recollection, and to gainsay completely the Countess Livia's instructions, involved, for him, an operation as drastic as that of a man chopping off his own fingers in suspicion of their infection with rabies. For any such operation courage would be required ; but when it is remembered that Woodseer, so far, had not been aware of receiving any bite, knew only what he had taken for a life-giving experience, the instant diagnosis and detection of the poison's existence is felt to be a quality rarer even than courage.

Fleetwood's errors are subtler, as his circumstances are more involved. Like Woodseer, and almost all the characters of distinction in the tale, he is Welsh. What, in his eyes, the possession of Welsh blood stands for, Meredith has been at pains in a good many places to inform his readers. During Victor Radnor's great concert, in *One of our Conquerors*, a German visitor has to hear comments from the audience that cause him to ask whether the English care in the least for music, or indeed for any immaterial good. Meredith replies to the question in person. The English, he says, do care for art rather more than appears ; moreover in speaking of them as a nation, it has to be realized how largely the mass now is being inspirited by the Welsh, Irish, and Scotch. In *Sandra Belloni* pride in his race is even more ardently expressed. He alludes there to ' peculiar Welsh delicacy ', and says, ' all subtle feelings are discovered by Welsh eyes, when untroubled by any mental agitation. Brother and sister were Welsh, and I may observe that there is human nature and Welsh nature.' And now, with reference to Fleetwood, he reminds us that a Welshman is excitable, ready at all times to start on a quest, a wild-goose chase even, but that, though his quarry may be vague and immaterial to the eyes of onlookers, it will be clear in his own. Unlike the Teuton, he tells us, the Welshman never kindles the fire of his present on the ashes of his past. Loved or hated, that which once has been for him lives animate behind the shroud, quick at a word, a scent, a sound, to reassert itself. This last trait is the key to much that is

otherwise puzzling in Fleetwood's career. For in
English natures at war with themselves it is a characteristic of their want of unity to be able to act in
their best moments in forgetfulness of their worst.
But Fleetwood is dogged throughout by memories
of actions so alien to his feeling in the present,
seemingly so little emanations of himself, that he
sinks back on the idea of fatality. He is roused to
a peculiarly keen consciousness of this in the scene
where he finally parts from his wife by the graveyard
of the very church where they had been married.
After long separation, he comes to the house he has
apportioned her, determined, whatever it may cost
him, to arrive at an understanding. Hearing he is
to come, Carinthia goes to stay with some friends
who live near by. Fleetwood accompanies her in
the late afternoon on her walk to their house. ' Up
the lane by the park they had open lands to the
heights of Croridge. " Splendid clouds," Fleetwood
remarked. She looked up, thinking of the happy long
day's walk with her brother to the Styrian Baths.
Pleasure in the sight made her face shine superbly.
" A flying Switzerland, Mr. Woodseer says," she
replied ; " England is beautiful on days like these.
For walking, I think the English climate very good.'
He dropped a murmur : " It should suit so good
a walker," and burned to compliment her spirited
easy stepping, and scorned himself for the sycophancy
it would be before they were on the common ground
of a restored understanding. But an approval of any
of her acts threatened him with enthusiasm for the
whole of them, her person included ; and a dam in

his breast had to keep back the flood. " You quote Woodseer to me, Carinthia. I wish you knew Lord Feltre. He can tell you of every cathedral, convent and monastery, in Europe and Syria. Nature is well enough ; she is, as he says, a savage. Men's works, acting under divine direction to escape from that tangle, are better worthy of study, perhaps. If one has done wrong, for example." " I could listen to him," she said. " You would not need—except, yes, one thing. Your father's book speaks of not forgiving an injury." " My father does. He thinks it weakness to forgive an injury. Women do, and they are disgraced, they are thought slavish. My brother is much stronger than I am. He is my father alive in that." " It is anti-Christian, some would think." " Let offending people go. He would not punish them. They may go where they will be forgiven. For them our religion is a happy retreat : we are glad they have it. My father and my brother say that injury forbids us to be friends again. My father was injured by the English Admiralty : he never forgave it ; but he would have fought one of their ships and offered his blood any day, if his country called to battle." . . . The dwarf tower of Croridge village church fronted them against the sky, seen of both. " You remember it," he said. And she answered : " I was married there." " You have not forgotten that injury, Carinthia ? " " I am a mother." " By all the saints ! you hit hard. Justly. Not you. Our deeds are the hard hitters. We learn when they begin to flagellate, stroke upon stroke ! Suppose we hold a costly thing in the hand and dash it to the ground— no recovering of it, none ! That must be what your

father meant. I can't regret you are a mother.
We have a son, a bond. How can I describe the man
I was ! " he muttered—" possessed ! sort of were-
wolf ! You are my wife ? " " I was married to you,
my lord." " It 's a tie of a kind." " It binds me."
" Obey, you said." " Obey *it*. I do." " You consider it holy ? " " My father and mother spoke to
me of the marriage-tie. I read the service before
I stood at the altar. It is holy. It is dreadful.
I will be true to it." " To your husband ? " " To
his name, to his honour." " To the vow to live with
him ? " " My husband broke that for me." " Carinthia, if he bids you, begs you to renew it ?
God knows what you may save me from." " Pray
to God. Do not beg of me, my lord. I have my
brother and my little son. No more of husband for
me ! God has given me a friend, too—a man of
humble heart, my brother's friend, my dear Rebecca's
husband. He can take them from me : no one but
God. See the splendid sky we have." With those
words she barred the gate on him ; at the same time
she bestowed the frank look of an amiable face
brilliant in the lively red of her exercise, in its bent-
bow curve along the forehead, out of the line of
beauty, touching as her voice was, to make an
undertone of anguish swell an ecstasy. So he felt
it, for his mood was now the lover's. A torture
smote him, to find himself transported by that voice
at his ear to the scene of the young bride in Thirty-
acre Meadow. " I propose to call on Captain Kirby-
Levellier to-morrow, Carinthia," he said. " The
name of the house ? " " My brother is not now any
more in the English army," she replied. " He has

hired a furnished house named Stoneridge." "He will receive me, I presume?" "My brother is a courteous gentleman, my lord." "Here is the church, and here we have to part for to-day. Do we?" "Good-bye to you, my lord," she said. He took her hand and dropped the dead thing. "Your idea is, to return to Esslemont some day or other?" "For the present," was her strange answer. She bowed, she stepped on. On she sped, leaving him at the stammering beginning of his appeal to her. Their parting by the graveyard of the church that had united them was what the world would class as curious. To him it was a further and a well-marked stroke of the fatality pursuing him.'

Standing for the last glimpse of the disappearing Carinthia, Fleetwood finds himself fingering a pocket pistol, borrowed from the relative of one of his satellites who lately committed suicide. He recalls talk of his Romanist friend, Lord Feltre, and he reflects that, if the church here at hand were a Roman church, he could enter and cleanse himself of the past in confession. Feltre says that two sexes at war with each other must abjure their sex to find peace; Woodseer, on the other hand, is all for regaining—outside the Church—the right to be numbered among the world's fighting men, "the *act* penitential, youth put behind us, the steady course ahead." The ideas are diametrically opposed, but, in real friendship for both these men, Fleetwood's conscience is awaking. With all his intimates but Feltre and Woodseer, Fleetwood had been handicapped by his wealth; having been 'accustomed to buy men and women' he early lost faith in their

ingenuousness. Since the day of his first meeting
with Woodseer in the Bavarian highlands, his
character has moved far and fast. His whimsical
feeling for Carinthia had darkened to bitterness
almost before their engagement, and from the
morning of their marriage they were never together
again, overtly, till the present struggle began. In
this struggle he has had cause for complaint, for
Carinthia has been strangely unimaginative. He
begins to suspect that she is not aware of the degree
in which she was thrust, by her relatives, on to her
lord ; none the less by her unsolicited championship
and pursuance of her husband she has put him in
situations so ridiculous that any man with a keen
social sense must have found them difficult to forgive.
However, for the long neglect, for the kidnapping,
and for an offence deeper and darker than these,
Carinthia's pardon has to be sought. And now
Fleetwood's love has developed, the reader is forced
to recognize that his feeling is more subtle and, in
some ways, too delicate for that of his wife. In fact,
given the main outlines of character—whimsical
subtlety and over-sensitiveness on one side, and
heroic simplicity and literalness on the other—the
situation is comprehensible enough.

But what Fleetwood failed to grasp till too late, and
what goes far to justify Carinthia's unimaginativeness,
is the heroic scale on which her nature is built. Devoid
of subtlety of perception, it is devoid also of small-
mindedness or shadow of turning. She has nothing in
common with the familiar type of character which
disclaims attention to other people's foibles while
demanding excessive sympathy for its own. In her

unquestioning acceptance of Fleetwood's silence and inaction from the night of the ball till the day of their wedding there is foolishness certainly, but there is also a grandeur, outlining and mirroring her own conception of constancy, that gives her rank with the greatest. To every woman worthy the name a passionate love must lend some access of single-mindedness and courage ; to such as Carinthia and Nesta, in whose hearts these virtues are native, there can in love's presence be no counting of costs. ' They sink back upon no breast of love ', they grasp at a flaming sword, but—a sword, and no plaything—its work may be to carve the way out of a fool's paradise. Mere reaction of feeling is hasty ; but change embracing the whole of a character is slow. It is, for Meredith, an integral part of Carinthia's greatness that she should move to her final position step by step and unwillingly. Overleaping of fences is not Carinthia's title to consideration, any more than it is Nesta's or Aminta's ; the qualities of all three are stable and independent of circumstance. Difference between a wise man and a fool probably lies less in the smaller number of mistakes of the wise man than in the fact that he will not fall into the same mistakes twice. Is it not impossible to conceive of Nataly or Countess Fanny, Aminta or Carinthia, as repeating their experiences ? In every case, indeed, the exact reverse is stated of them. Their freedom is achieved as a means to an end. And in this—the fact that their quest is for righteousness and wisdom, not for any renewal of sensation, however exalted—is the secret of their peculiar and permanent beauty.

CHAPTER XIV

SOME THOUGHTS IN CONCLUSION
LAST YEARS, 1895–1909

IN concluding this review of the novels, the Old
Buccaneer's 'Maxims for Men' brings us back to
the point where we began with 'The Pilgrim's Scrip'
of *Richard Feverel*—to Meredith's partiality for what
we may call the element of the Chorus in fiction.   In
ancient Greek Tragedy the detachment of the Chorus
allowed indulgence in almost unlimited sententious-
ness without the sermonizing element being brought
within the drama itself.   It admitted also speech that
was both poetically and philosophically at a pitch
different from that of human talk.   As I set forth
in my introductory chapter, George Meredith at the
beginning of his work had decided that for him to
write a novel excluding philosophy would be ' to bid
a pumpkin caper '.   He had, that is, to be a thinker.
How then was he to escape being a preacher ?   The
philosophical element, clearly, must be introduced by
some sleight of hand.   So, instead of improving
remarks being made *in propria persona*, some grey-
headed senior had to be impelled to produce a book
of his long-ago published proverbs, or some hitherto
neglected manuscript by an unknown author was
discovered.   Such was the recurrent superficial aspect
of Meredith's favourite thesis that fiction can only be
developed with the aid of philosophy.   The deeper
aspect comes from the core of his work.   ' Philosophy ',

he says, ' is required to make our human nature creditable and acceptable. Fiction implores you to heave a bigger breast and take her in with this heavenly preservative helpmate, her inspiration and her essence.' What, after all, was the main value of the old Greek Chorus, if not that it provided, as well by the dignity as by the detachment of its utterances, a spiritual atmosphere, in which the significance of events passing upon the stage could be realized in their relation to a truth outliving them ; that it called upon spectators of the tragedy to view the actors and incidents presented, not only in their particular, but in their universal aspect—to ' heave a bigger breast ' ? In short, the Chorus points us to that high post of vantage at which the visions of poet and philosopher coalesce ; and it is Meredith's greatness in his novels that he so frequently attains to it.

Upon minor characteristics and partialities in George Meredith's work a book might be written. A few only that are outstanding can be touched upon here. Among them is his peculiar affection for a south-west wind. His devotion to that is due, first, to the fact that it is so prevalent in England ; Redworth, in *Diana of the Crossways*, says that if you consult old calendars you will discover that they give south-west weather an average of seven months of the English year. This—the plain fact of its being— would, to Meredith, be ground enough for friendliness. But the manly strength of the south-west, its womanly variableness, the perennial freshness that accompanies it in earth and sky, further endear it to him. And his delight in these qualities may be traced from the first of his novels to the latest. The time of day at which Fleetwood and Carinthia passed out of Esslemont gates on their last walk together, Meredith tells us, not by his watch, but by consulting the sky, ' at that hour of the late afternoon when south-westerly breezes, after a summer gale, drive their huge white flocks over blue fields fresh as morning, on the march to pile the crown of the sphere, and end a troubled day with grandeur '. And of that culminating grandeur *The Ordeal of Richard Feverel* had, nearly forty years before, given the description. ' The wind had dropped, the clouds had rolled from the zenith and ranged in amphitheatre with distant flushed bodies over sea and land : Titanic crimson head and chest rising from the wave faced Hyperion falling. There hung Briareus with deep-indented trunk and ravined brows, stretching all his hands up to unattainable blue summits. North-west the range had a rich white glow, as if shining to the moon, and westward, streams of amber, melting into the upper rose, shot out from the dipping disk.' *The South-West Wind in the Woodland* had been in the poems of 1851 ; the 1862 volume had contained the apostrophe to the south-west of the *Ode to the Spirit of Earth in Autumn* ; and *A Reading of Earth* in 1888 had produced *The South-Wester* with all the magnificent faithfulness of its imagery :

> Day of the cloud in fleets !   O day
> Of wedded white and blue, that sail
> Immingled, with a footing ray
> In shadow-sandals down our vale !—
> And swift to ravish golden meads,
> Swift up the run of turf it speeds,

> They bright of head and dark of heel ;
> To where the hill-top flings on sky,
> As hawk from wrist or dust from wheel,
> The tiptoe scalers tossed to fly.

Those are the poem's opening lines. Near to its close
we have :

> Only at gathered eve knew we
> The marvels of the day : for then
> Mount upon mountain out of sea
> Arose, and to our spacious ken
> Trebled sublime Olympus round
> In towering amphitheatre.
> Colossal on enormous mound
> Majestic gods we saw confer.

And the similarity of these last lines to the *Richard
Feverel* passage brings us to another of Meredith's
characteristics. Having received the incisive impression and found the image to carry it, he felt no
scruple about employing that image more than once.
The telling expression in the *Hymn to Colour*, ' We
came where woods breathed sharp,' is recollected
from *The Ordeal of Richard Feverel*, and the equally
notable expression about horned rocks which immediately succeeds it in the *Hymn* echoes a passage of
Farina. In fact, no one well acquainted with the
novels can read the poems without feeling that they
are, in one aspect, the novels in distillation. Who
doubts that *Love in the Valley* was written by Richard
for Lucy, or that the nightingales singing in that
magical *Night of Frost in May* are the same as those
with which Emilia matched herself, or that the
sunrise of the *Hymn to Colour* was Carinthia's
sunrise ?

So keen an observer as Meredith, inevitably, had his favourites among birds and flowers. Of birds, after the lark, nightingale, and thrush, the tits claimed his attention ; the night-jar is several times described sitting on a pine-branch with a star over his head ; and the great green woodpecker snapshotted as he breaks from cover uttering his melodious cry. Among flowers, after the wild-cherry tree, the pale autumn crocus took first place in his mind. Its earliest appearance is in *Farina* when Margarita wears it, bell downwards, in her hair ; and both in *Diana of the Crossways* and in *The Amazing Marriage* our attention is called to the beauty of it when growing in a mass. A different crocus, but still a crocus, at the end of *The Thrush in February* provides perhaps the most lovely image in the whole range of Meredith's poetry. Swimming, which to Meredith was so ecstatic a pleasure, takes a considerable place both in the novels and the poems. The swimming scene which forms the climax in *Lord Ormont* occurs most directly to our minds ; but hardly less constant in memory are certain metaphorical uses such as Clara's dive in view of the looming breaker of Willoughby Patterne's embrace, or the

> Enter these enchanted woods,
>   You who dare.
> Nothing harms beneath the leaves
> More than waves a swimmer cleaves

of *The Woods of Westermain*, or

> When the pleasures, like waves to a swimmer,
> Come heaving for rapture ahead

in the *Ode to Youth in Memory*.

In the preceding chapter, when we were considering *The Amazing Marriage*, we dwelt at some length upon the description of dawn on the morning that Carinthia was saying farewell to her childhood's home, noting connexion between that description and the *Hymn to Colour*. No student of Meredith's writing can doubt that the *Hymn* is, like the prose passage, telling us not of dawn only, but of dawn among mountains. Of what was, in Meredith's youth and prime manhood, not less than a passion for walking I have spoken already, and for him, as for Leslie Stephen, leader of 'The Tramps', joy of the pedestrian grew to ecstasy among mountains. Indeed, we come here on a matter that those who have cared deeply for George Meredith cannot find easy to speak of. To them, certain letters that passed between Meredith and Stephen at the end of the year 1903 and the beginning of 1904 possess a ring of the *Odyssey*. In August of 1903 Meredith, able again to hold a pen after months of incapacity, writes to Leslie Stephen that Marie Sturgis is visiting in a high mountain villa close to a glacier on which she disports herself, and that she is going on from there to St. Moritz. What, he asks, does Stephen experience in face of such reports of mountain activities from his young ones ? The pangs he, George Meredith, feels are acute, even though within five minutes his philosophy can reassert itself. The only response that Stephen was able to make to that letter comes from a region comment may not enter ; the words must be given entire—' My very dear friend, I must make the effort to write to you once more with my own hand. I cannot trust anyone else to say how much I value your friendship, and I must send you a message, perhaps it may be my last, of my satisfaction and pride in thinking of your affection for me. Your bunch of violets is deliciously scenting my prisonhouse.' On the 14th February Meredith wrote back: ' My dearest Leslie, Your letter gave me one of the few remaining pleasures that I can have. I rejoice in your courage and energy. Of the latter I have nothing left. Since last September I have not held a pen, except perforce to sign my name. We who have loved the motion of legs and the sweep of the winds,[1] we come to this. But for myself I will own that it is the natural order. There is no irony in Nature. God bless and sustain you, my friend.' Six days later Leslie Stephen was dead; he had been suffering long from internal cancer. Of these two men's voices hardly can we discern which is the voice of Ulysses: ' one equal temper of heroic hearts.' Stephen himself, however, would have felt small patience with such questioning. To him, George Meredith, noble walker and swimmer and devotee of boxing, intimate of the sun and stars, was of the Heroes in bodily as well as in mental capacity. Hyndman has said of Meredith's physique that he was all wire and whipcord; Burnand has commented, ' George never walked, never lounged; he strode, he took giant strides '. Vividly good-looking, with thick reddish hair, the appearance of George Meredith as a young man is preserved to us in the

---

[1] Leslie Stephen in 1860 at Cambridge had won the University Mile, and walked from Cambridge to London (50 miles) in twelve hours. He had coached his college boat. From 1865 to 1868 he had been President of the Alpine Club.

Christ of Dante Gabriel Rossetti's ' Mary Magdalene
at the Gate of Simon the Pharisee '.   With sonorous
voice, resounding laugh, and a born tease, the first
word and the last regarding him as a person should
be of his gusto—his immense, boyish, love of absurdities.   His range of enjoyment was very great.
A connoisseur of wines and cigars and something of
an epicure, he was a considerable linguist, and cared
very deeply for music.   I have spoken in this book of
one of his characters as having the windows of his
soul wide open to life and its lessons.   Meredith's
nature was, the whole of it, window.   His difficulty
in his art was that he could not confine himself to an
angle of vision ; that he refracted from all sides at
once.   Each experience made an impress on his
sensitiveness ; every sensation he was conscious of was
intellectualized, and onward from the day of *Modern
Love* and *Richard Feverel* most of these, when brain-
spun, were woven to the brocades of his books.   How
homogeneous indeed were his life and his writings
became fully discernible only when, in 1912, his son
published *The Letters of George Meredith.*

Public appreciation, though it came to him late,
came to George Meredith unequivocally [1] in the last
years of his life.   In 1892 he received the LL.D. of

[1] For a moment, indeed, just at the time of Meredith's death,
what had seemed to my generation to be thrice-dead contro-
versies did bestir themselves in the Dean's refusal to allow
George Meredith's interment in Westminster Abbey—a refusal
given in face of a personal request from Edward the Seventh and
a petition including the name of almost every notable English
writer then living.   A Memorial Service, however, was held in the
Abbey on the day that Meredith's ashes were buried, beside his
wife, in Dorking Cemetery—23 May 1909.

St. Andrews University, and the same year he was
elected President of the Society of Authors. In 1902
he became Vice President of the London Library.
In 1905 he received the Order of Merit, and the
(rarely bestowed) Gold Medal of the Royal Society
of Literature. The Order of Merit, valuable to him
partly because it constituted him what he called
'a Brother Merit' to his deeply-loved friend John
Morley, was by King Edward's command conferred
upon him in his own house at Box Hill. The considerate kindness of that arrangement—he had of
course at first been summoned to Windsor to be
invested with the Insignia—touched and pleased
Meredith particularly. For in 1899 he had been
obliged to refuse the offer of an honorary degree from
the University of Oxford because the rule of atten-
dance to receive it could not be waived. To the
outpouring of affection and admiration, particularly
from younger members of his own profession, that
came to him on the occasion of his eightieth birthday
—in February of 1908—I have alluded in my introductory chapter.

On the 13th April 1909 he wrote the last letter he
ever was to write, on hearing of Swinburne's death.
Growingly absorbed in questionings as to the nature
of death, George Meredith's piercing perception of the
vividness that was extinct in Swinburne's grave,
would, in view of his own swiftly following end, press
on us too sharply, had we not always memory of
a letter of his of New Year's Night, 1877. 'I greet
you', he then said to John Morley, 'in the first hour
of the New Year, after a look at the stars from my

chalet door, and listening to the bells. We have just marked one of our full stops, at which Time, turning back as he goes, looks with his old-gentleman smile. To come from a gaze at the stars—Orion and shaking Sirius below him—is to catch a glance at the inscrutable face of him that hurries us on, as on a wheel, from dust to dust. I thought of you and how it might be with you this year : hoped for good : saw beyond good and evil to great stillness, another form of moving for you and me. It seems to me that Spirit is—how, where, and by what means involving us, none can say. But in this life there is no life save in the spirit. The rest of life, and we may know it in love, is an aching and rotting.' On Sunday night, the 16th of May 1909, he was taken ill, and, on the next morning but one, conscious almost to the end, he moved into the stillness, at dawn. For a quarter of a century he had been an outstanding figure of English literary life ; for a number of those years he had been supreme in it. But the point I wish to reiterate here is that when he went from us he went ahead— still leading in thought : we called into that sunrise after him, ' HE 'S FOR THE MORNING.'

NOTE

IN 1910 and 1911 the *Memorial Edition* of Meredith's works was published, in twenty-seven volumes (by Messrs. Constable in England and Messrs. Charles Scribner's Sons in New York). This edition contains an unfinished story of 224 pages, *Celt and Saxon* (in volume xx) ; *The Sentimentalists*, a comedy begun in 1863 ; and *The Gentleman of Fifty and the Damsel of Nineteen* (both the two last in volume xxii, with *The House on the Beach*). The reason I have not discussed these fragments in the text of this book may be discovered by any inquirer from a letter of George Meredith's written on the 7th of September 1907 respecting a bibliography made by Mr. A. Esdaile.

The most complete bibliography, both of Meredith's own works, and of other people's writings about them, is to be found in the two volumes prepared by Mr. Maurice Buxton Forman and issued in 1922 and 1924, by the Dunedin Press of Edinburgh, for the Bibliographical Society.

INDEX

A

Allegory (*The Shaving of Shagpat*), 19–25.
Amazing Marriage, The, 207 (note), 214, 216–32, 237, 238.
Appreciation, 175.
Arabian Entertainment, An (*The Shaving of Shagpat*), 19–25.
Arabian Nights, The, 16, 19.
Austria, 114.
Austro-Italian War of 1866, 90.

B

Ballad of Fair Ladies in Revolt, 200.
Ballad of Past Meridian, The, 3, 185.
Ballads and Poems of Tragic Life, 174.
Beauchamp's Career, 3–4, 113–26, 158.
Berne, 107.
Bismarck, Count, 97–8.
Blake, William, 184.
Breath of the Briar, 189.
Bright, John, 115, 116.
Browning, Robert, 14, 68; quotation from, 242.
Buch der Lieder, 187.
Burden of Strength, The, 151.
Burnand, Sir Francis, 174, 239.
Burns, Robert, 131, 187.
Byron, Lord, 118, 215.

C

Cambridge, 43, 239.
Carlyle, Thomas, 43, 119, 125–6.

Case of General Ople and Lady Camper, The, 144.
Catherine of Siena, St., 25.
Celt and Saxon, 243.
Changes caused by War of 1914–18, 1.
Change in Recurrence, 174.
Charnock, Richard Stephen, 16.
Chelsea, 29.
Chorus, Greek, 233–4.
Clarissa (Richardson), 85–6.
Clark, Mrs. (Edith Nicolls), 192, 199.
Cobden, Life of Richard (J. Morley), 114.
Comedy, Essay on, 7, 127–31, 141.
Comic Spirit, The, 21–3, 46, 129–35, 148–9.
Comic Spirit, Ode to the, 185.
Constable, Messrs., prefatory note and appendix.
Constant Nymph, The, 222.
Consulate and the Empire, The, 98.
Conway, Moncure, 113.
Copsham, 19, 43, 50, 51, 53, 70.
Courage, Gospel of, 4–7.
Crimea, 114–5, 119.
Crotchet Castle, 137–8.

D

Day of the Daughter of Hades, The, 190–1.
Diana of the Crossways, 151, 161–73, 192, 214, 234, 237.
Dickens, Charles, 2, 16.
Dönniges, Helène von (Frau von Racowitza), 148–58.

Dorking, 2, 158, 240.
Duff-Gordon, Janet (Ross), 19, 50, 51, 77.
Dyspepsia, Meredith's suffering from, 43, 111.

E

Earth's Secret, 175, 176.
Edward the Seventh, King, 240, 241.
Egoist, The, 13, 38, 50, 77, 122, 131–41, 167, 216.
Eightieth Birthday, Meredith's, 2, 241.
Eliot, George, 3, 19, 20, 68.
Elliot, Miss (Mrs. W. M. Meredith), 207.
Empty Purse, The, 5, 8, 47, 50, 222.
Esher, 18, 44, 50.
Essay on Comedy, 7, 127–31, 141.
Evan Harrington, 44–51, 79.
Evans, Elizabeth E. (*Ferdinand Lassalle and Helène von Dönniges, A Modern Tragedy*), 152.
Evian, 161.

F

Faith on Trial, A, 137, 174, 175.
Farina, 25–8, 236, 237.
Fiction, Meredith's philosophy of, 8, 9, 11, 89, 134–5, 149, 233–4.
Fortnightly Review, The, 7, 89, 98, 113, 158, 161, 175, 186.
France, Ode to, 98, 99.
Franco-Prussian War, 95–100.
Frost on the May Night, 70, 80.

G

Gentleman of Fifty, The, 243.
German character, 97, 99–100, 106.

Germany, school-days of Meredith in, 16.
Gibbon, 128.
Giusti, 187.
Goethe, 187.
Gryll Grange, 137–8.

H

Halliford, Lower, 17, 18.
Hamble Water, 81, 113.
Hamlet, 92, 104.
Hard Weather, 178.
Hardman, William, 52, 70, 82, 89, 114.
Hardy, Thomas, 29, 149, 174.
Harry Richmond, 38, 100–6.
Harvard University, 192.
Heine, Heinrich, 156, 187.
Herbert, Sidney, 162.
House on the Beach, The, 141–4.
Hymn to Colour, 12, 184–6, 236, 238.
Hyndman, 239.

I

Idea of Comedy and the Uses of the Comic Spirit, The, 127–31.
Ipswich Journal, The, 43.
Italian Independence, 89–95.

J

James, Henry, 3, 14.
Jessopp, Augustus, 16, 43, 53–4, 68, 107, 108.
Juggling Jerry, 70.
Jump-to-Glory Jane, 198.

K

Keats, John, 183.
Kingsley, Charles, 17.
Kossuth, Louis, 114.

L

Lark Ascending The, 175, 178–81.
Lassalle, Ferdinand, 148–58.

Lassalle and Helène von Dön-niges, 152 note.
Lassalle, Meine Beziehungen zu Ferdinand, 148 note.
Lewis, G. H., 89.
London Library,Meredith Vice-President of, 241.
Lord Ormont and his Aminta, 207–16, 237.
Love in the Valley, 188–9, 236.
Lytton, Robert, 186.

M

Manchester School, The, 116, 119, 125–6.
Masefield, John, 70.
Maxse, Frederick, 18, 43, 44, 68, 81, 82, 89, 97, 99, 107, 109, 113–4, 120, 125, 161.
Mazzini, Giuseppe, 91–3.
McKechnie, James, 20, 21, 23.
McNamara, Jane (Mrs. Augustus Meredith), 15.
Memorial service, Westminster Abbey, 2, 240.
Memorial Edition of George Meredith's Works, 243.
MEREDITH, GEORGE ; parentage, 15 ; school-days, 15–16 ; articled to solicitor, 16 ; conversational powers and first literary efforts, 16 ; friendship with Peacock family, 16–17 ; marriage to Thomas Love Peacock's daughter, 17 ; first volume of Poems, 17 ; shared house with Peacock ; eldest son born, 17 ; estrangement from his wife, 18 ; took his baby son to London lodgings, 18 ; returned to Esher, 18 ; went to Copsham to be near Duff-Gordons, 19 ; first fiction, 19–28 ; first novel, 29–43 ; ill-health combated by exercise, 43 ; journalist work, 43 ; Thomas Carlyle's praise of *The Ordeal of Richard Feverel*, 43 ; friendships with literary men, 43 ; continued ill-health and depression, 50 ; travel in Switzerland, Italy, and France,with son, Arthur, 51 ; wife's last illness and death, 51–2 ; and effect on Arthur, 52–3 ; arranged Arthur should go to King Edward VI Grammar School, Norwich, 54 ; Swinburne's championship of *Modern Love*, 54 ; Browning's praise of Poems and Meredith's description of his own attitude to poetry-writing, 68–9 ; the Vulliamy family, 81 ; Mickleham, 81 ; marriage to Miss Marie Vulliamy, 81 ; birth of son William Maxse Meredith, 89 ; Italian correspondent of the *Morning Post*, 90 ; Swinburne's praise of *Vittoria*, 90 ; writings about Franco-Prussian War, 95–100 ; anxieties about Arthur's future, 107–11 ; birth of Marie Eveleen Meredith, 109 ; superficial irritability from ill-health, 111 ; work for Fred Maxse's Radical candidature at Southampton in 1867, 113 ; lectured at The London Institution, 127 ; caught whooping-cough from Will and Marie, 158 ; better and able to entertain the 'Sunday Tramps', 158 ; Will Meredith attending Westminster School, 159 ; Arthur Meredith ill at Lille, 159 ; George Meredith's concern for Arthur, 159–60 ; treatment for an affection of the spine, 161 ; douches at Avalon, and travel with Arthur in Italy, 161 ; fame from *Diana of the Crossways*, 161 ; illness,

and death, of wife, 173–4 ; travail of mind, 174–5 ; Arthur sent on voyage to Australia, 192 ; fame in America and praises from Harvard, 192 ; Will Meredith's marriage, 207 ; visits to Loseley Hall, 207 ; anxieties about completion of his work, 207 ; Marie Meredith's marriage, 207 ; last letters to Leslie Stephen, 238–9 ; suffering from loss of physical power, 238 ; portrait of Meredith's young manhood by D. G. Rossetti, 240 ; general public appreciation, 240–2 ; last letter on news of Swinburne's death, 241.

Meredith, Arthur (George Meredith's son), 17, 43, 51, 52–4, 107–11, 159–61, 192, 199.
—, Anne Eliza, 15.
—, Augustus (George Meredith's father), 15.
—, Catherine Matilda, 15.
—, Harriet, 15.
—, Jane, 15.
—, Louisa, 15.
—, Marie (George Meredith's wife), 81, 89, 107, 173, 174.
—, Marie Eveleen (George Meredith's daughter), 109, 158, 174, 207, 238.
—, Mary Ellen (George Meredith's wife), 17, 51, 52.
—, Melchisedek (George Meredith's grandfather), 15.
—, William Maxse, prefatory note, 89, 158, 159, 174, 207.
Modern Love, 9–10, 12, 18, 52, 54–67, 68, 69, 75, 114, 129, 190, 240.
Molière, 134.
Moravian School, 16.
Morison, Cotter, 97, 127, 159.
—, Theodore, 159.
Morley, John, 3, 95, 100, 108, 113, 114, 161, 174, 199, 241.

Morley, Mrs. John, 174.
Morning Post, The (Meredith Italian correspondent of), 90.
Musset, Alfred de, 187.
My Theme, 175.

N

Napoleon the First, 99.
Napoleon, Louis, 114.
Napoleonic tradition, 96–7.
Neuer Früling, 187.
Neuwied, 16.
New Year's Night, 1877, 241.
Nicholas the First, 115.
Nicolls, Edith (Mrs. Clark), 17, 192, 199.
Nicolls, Mary Ellen (Mrs. George Meredith), 17, 51, 52.
Night of Frost in May, 178, 182, 236.
Nonancourt, 98, 174.
Norton, Mrs. Caroline, 161–2.
Norwich, 16, 52, 53, 54, 107.

O

Obscurity, 8, 12–14.
Ode to the Comic Spirit, 127–31, 185.
Ode to France, 98, 99.
Ode to the South-Wester, 178, 183, 235–6.
Ode of the Spirit of Earth in Autumn, 70, 235.
Ode to Youth in Memory, 237.
Odyssey, The, 238.
Old Chartist, The, 70.
One of our Conquerors, 10–11, 38, 88, 192–9, 207, 226.
Orchard and the Heath, The, 190.
Ordeal of Richard Feverel, The, 1, 29–43, 71, 74, 85, 134, 233, 235, 236, 240.
Order of Merit (invested with the insignia at Box Hill), 241.
Outer and Inner, 176–8, 181–2.
Oxford, University of, 241.

P

Palmer, General, 207.
Palmerston, Lord, 114.
Pattison, Mark, 19.
Peacock, Ned, 16.
—, Thomas Love, 16, 17, 18 (see *Crotchet Castle* and *Gryll Grange*, 137–8).
Peel, Sir Robert, 162.
Peterborough, Earl of, 207.
Phaéthôn, 189.
Pilgrim's Progress, The, 19, 20.
Poems of 1851, 17, 183.
Poems of 1862 (*Poems of the English Roadside*), 68–70.
Poems and Lyrics of the Joy of Earth, 161, 175.
Political views, Meredith's, 3–5.
Portsmouth, 15, 44.
Prelude, The, 2.

Q

Quakers, The, 115.

R

Racowitza, Frau von (Helène von Dönniges), 148–58.
Reading of Earth, A, 174, 176, 235.
Rhoda Fleming, 81–8, 193.
Richardson, Samuel, 85–6.
Robinson, Anastasia, 208.
Ross, Janet (Duff-Gordon), 19, 50, 51, 77.
Rossetti, D. G., 43, 143, (Portrait of Meredith) 240.
—, W. M., 17, 43, 183.
Royal Society of Literature, Gold Medal of, 241.
Ruskin, John, 25.
Russia, 114–5.

S

Sage Enamoured and The Honest Lady, The, 66, 114, 199–206.
Salvation Army, the, 198.

Sandra Belloni (*Emilia in England*), 29, 38, 48, 51, 70–80, 89–91, 93, 134, 216, 226.
Sélincourt, Basil de, 176 (see Prefatory note).
Sentimentalist, The, 243.
Sermon to our Later Prodigal Son (*The Empty Purse*), 5, 8, 47, 50, 222.
Shaving of Shagpat, The, 19–25, 28.
Shelley, Percy Bysshe, 178, 179, 187.
Sheridan, Richard Brinsley, 161.
Society of Authors, Meredith President of, 241.
South-West Wind, 234–6.
South-West Wind in the Woodland, The, 235.
South-Wester, Ode to the, 178, 183, 235.
Spencer, Herbert, 29.
Spirit of Earth in Autumn, Ode to the, 70, 235.
St. Andrews University (Meredith, LL.D. of), 241.
Stephen, Leslie, 158, 238–9.
Stevenson, Robert Louis, 40, 158, 174.
Sturge, Joseph, 115.
Sturgis, Henry Parkman, 207.
—, Mrs. (Marie Meredith), 109, 158, 174, 207, 238.
Stuttgart, 96, 107, 109.
Sunday Tramps, 158.
Surrey, Scenery of, 29.
Swift, 128.
Swinburne, Algernon, 43, 54, 80, 90, 183, 241.

T

Tale of Chloe, The, 27, 134, 141, 144–7.
Taylor, Tom, 160.
Tennyson, Alfred, 187, 188.
Test of Manhood, The, 185.

Thackeray, W. M., 2.
Thiers, Louis Adolphe, 97–8.
Thomson, James, 42, 137.
Thrush in February, The, 178, 190, 237.
Tragic Comedians, The, 120, 148–58.
Trevelyan, George, 92, 120–1.
Tsar, Nicholas I, 115.
Two Masks, The, 135.

U

Ulysses, 239.

V

Valencia, 207.
Venice, 76, 79, 90, 89–95.
Vittoria, 76, 79, 89–95.
Vulliamy, the family, 81, 98, 108, 161.

Vulliamy, Marie (Mrs. George Meredith), 81, 173, 194.

W

War of 1914–18, gulf made by, 1.
Wellington, Duke of, 114.
Weybridge, 17, 18, 52.
White Monkey, The, 1.
Woking, 199.
Woodland Peace, 189.
Woods of Westermain, The, 6–7, 182, 237.
World's Advance, The, 203.
Wordsworth, William, 2, 177, 181.

Y

Young Italy, 93.
Youth in Memory, Ode to, 237.